THE MAN WE SERVE

Value Base of Human Services

Paul K.H. Kim

School of Social Work
Southern Illinois University

UNIVERSITY
PRESS OF
AMERICA

LANHAM • NEW YORK • LONDON

Copyright © 1977 by

University Press of America,™ Inc.

4720 Boston Way
Lanham, MD 20706

3 Henrietta Street
London WC2E 8LU England

ISBN (Perfect): 0-8191-0080-3

To my Great Mentors

ERNEST F. WITTE

WALTER L. KINDELSPERGER

TABLE OF CONTENTS

Since man is the object of human services and since concepts of man are the foundations of human services, man effectively influences the helping professions of law, medicine, nursing, education, social work, religion, and so on.

Historically, the world of man once consisted of "man of survival competition" and "man of mechanistic totality," and more recently "man of animal" and "man of libido." The world of man, however, is again entertaining a Biblical, humanistic, or democratic view of man, looking at man as "who he is" as well as "what he is." This humanistic view of man seeks the essences of man which are the roots of the various existences of man. The existences of man can be perceived objectively since they are within the sphere of the human reality of objectivity. On the contrary, the essences of man are original and beyond operational objectification by human perception. The essences lie beyond the human reality of objectivity -- in the human reality of appreciation and gratitude. Human essences are "there" as being simple man, making human existences possible to be and to become. They are "there" as the "given" divine endowments, as the permanent, absolute and unchanging nature, and as the universal element of all man regardless of "what he is."

This book therefore is to conceptualize "who man is" based on Biblical and humanistic existentialism, and on humanistic psychology, and is to delineate major essences of man which ought to be the fundamental premises of the professions of human services: Human dignity, human creativity, human freedom, human morality,and human proaction. This author admits, however, that human essences are more emphasized in this book than human existences. This is done with no intention of repudiating the human natures of existence, but rather because of age of technological advance and scientific social services.

In the process of completing this book, I have accumulated a debt of love and gratitude to a great many people who gave incalculable assistance and encouragement. Despite such a small product as this, I am unspeakably grateful for the product since it has become "I and me."

The author would like to express a sincere gratitude to the following persons: Dr. Esther B. McBride, Dean Fred M. Southerland, and Dr. Raymond W. Swan of the Tulane University School of Social Work, who served the dissertation committee with their valuable time and insightful stimulation; Ms. Linda Patrick of Southern Illinois University College of Human Resources, who made the typing of the manuscript possible; and Dr. Foster Brown, a fellow faculty member, who gave most generously his time for proof reading. In addition, the author is indebted to two most gracious and respectable mentors, Dr. Walter L. Kindelsperger and Dr. Ernest F. Witte, for their most valuable consultation, understanding, and concern.

"Think Creatively, Do Responsibly, and Love Powerfully." This should be the motto of the professions for human services today and tomorrow, and the days to come.

Chapter I

INTRODUCTION: THE WORLD IN CHANGE

Human life consists of sequential urges--that is, wishing and hoping for "newness" "betterness," and "difference." The course of human history has been to discover new knowledge to conquer little understood human phenomena, and as a consequence, new knowledge is incessantly being discovered and sometimes becomes a significant addition to human history. By virtue of such human knowledge, man today has the privilege of a more comfortable mechanized life than men of yesterday, as well as the challenge of facing new human problems--social, economic, psychological, educational and political problems which are seemingly "byproducts" of the human activity of discovery. In short, human life through time changes due to human activities in discovering.

One of the most significant human discoveries in the twentieth century is the computer, with its related technologies. Computer science is constantly growing, and introduces into human phenomena power hitherto unattainable by computerizing social systems such as political systems, economic systems, educational systems, engineering systems, and even the human individual system, focusing "on man's adjustment to society, on conformity and adaptation, on man as a controlled product of society and culture rather than a determiner of his own fate."[1] Computerization also helps man to deal with complexities of decision-making, planning and communication. Even in the medical profession computer medicine is under serious experiment. As Churchman writes, technological omnipotency for the provision of adequate medical care, sufficient education, human freedom, and better society in the absence of poverty and illegitimate violence, has its sacred recognition today.[2]

Ironically, however, a human plantive cry re-echoes around the world; many human beings, rich and poor, cry for "tomorrow," a healthier tomorrow than today--psychologically, physically, educationally, socially and economically. Such human dissatisfaction truly appears to be the byproduct of their lives in a world where there is the means being transformed into the ends itself; where the production and consumption of things have become the aims and values of life, and increased physical power has been valued more than an accumulated wisdom; where operationalism, individualism and independence rather than

1

interdependence, have become highly valued; where things act like men, and men are coerced to act like things; and where the identity of man is replaced by numerals transformed into a computerized identity. The world we live in is as though there exists much hate in the name of love, much riot in the name of peace, much divisiveness in the name of unity, and much "technological poverty, unemployment and warfare" in the name of technological panacea.[5]

Unavoidably then, there is a "sudden" twentieth century thirst for what Abraham Maslow names "B-value"--love, peace, revised newness, creativity, and so on--in the hearts of men today.[4] Some seek such B-value through communal living, through drug abuse, through losing self in psychedelic designs and rhythms, through religious meditation, through study of human psychology, and through self-destructive behavior such as suicide.[5] All these behaviors seem related to the searching for, and the hoped-for restoration of, man's lost identity in the state of "pulverization" and "robot."[6]

Science of Man: Psychology

What, for example, has been happening in the science of psychology, the sole purpose of which is to study human behavior?

Two major traditional schools of psychology, as mentioned by Gordon Allport in his provocative book Becoming are the Lockean tradition and Leibnitzian tradition. According to Allport, the Lockean tradition is rooted in a theoretical assumption that the human mind is born as a tabula rasa--merely a passing thing acquiring content and structure only through the impact of sensation and the crisscross of associations. Such thinking is found in associationism (sensory plus perceptual elements), environmentalism, behaviorism, stimulus-response (S-R) psychology, positivism and operationalism. All have contributed to the development of "scientific psychology, animal psychology and mathematical psychology," which treat the human being as a merely reactive organism. Their major premises are: (a) what is external and visible is more fundamental than what is not, and cause remains external to the organism; (b) what is small and molecular (simple ideas) is more fundamental than what is large and molar (complex ideas); and (c) what is earlier is more fundamental than what is late in development.

In contrast, the Leibnitzian tradition treats the human being as a self-propelled organism, and accordingly suggests an

2

inappropriateness of the S-R paradigm in comprehending human beings. The major theme of the Leibnitzian tradition is that human behavior is purposive, intellectual, righteous, and rational; and, therefore, to understand what a person is, it is necessary always to refer to what he may be in the future, for every state of the person is pointed in the direction of future possibilities. It is likely impossible then to classify and objectively measure human behavior. Freud's structural and libido-oriented psychoanalysis is rooted in the Lockean tradition and cognitive psychology, motivation theory, gestalt psychology, and humanistic psychology in the Leibnitzian tradition.[7]

Optimistic with the apparent fruits of the natural science, some scientists such as Pavlov, Skinner and Thorndike developed a hopeful strategy for direct application of natural sciences to the science of man. Their discipline is academically named "explicit behaviorism," which studies man within the framework of the S-R paradigm, and was further extended recently to "crypto- behaviorism," which studies man as "an information-processing entity operating on the principles of a binary digital computer programmed to conform to pay off criteria."[8] Both, however, equally eliminate the uniqueness and meaning of human subjective experiences as well as the generative, imaginative, judicial, and symbolic operation of the human mind.

Additionally, explicit or crypto-behaviorism (known as the first force in psychology) studies man based on an unchangeable philosophical assumption that man is the same as "a skinned-off lion" in terms of the principles of bodily function and physiological metabolism, except for man's superiority in employing "the greater complexities of verbal behavior."[9] It denounces the issues of human freedom by claiming that human freedom is nothing but a myth; in the process of scientific study of man, human freedom should be repudiated, but man has no freedom even to repudiate. In other words, behaviorism operates under the principle of determinism which claims that human behavior is "determined by the forces which are independent of the will."[10] Another important principle of behaviorism is "physical law and category of rationality," which are drawn from "the curve of normal distribution"--the scientific assumption generally accepted as the basis of universal phenomena.[11] With no exception, the human being and his behavior are subject to be classified, evaluated and described within the operation of the principles of the normal curve, and further subject to be controlled to "fit" under the given curve system by "stimulation" and "response."

In the late nineteenth century, Sigmund Freud was able to add human psychic phenomena to behaviorism and developed psychoanalysis, known as the second force in psychology. However, Freud and neo-Freudians appear to have a theoretical conceptualization of man, "man in war between self and world"--helpless victim of inner push and outer pull.[12] They have emphasized the man of pessimism, depression and aggression. Furthermore, their study of man has been involved in a structure of human personality rather than an image of human being; namely, Freudians have fragmented the human being into three basic constitutionalicies--id, ego and superego. According to Nameche, "id" is described as instinctive, aggressive, sexual drive and life energy (libido); and "ego" as the slave of three harsh masters (id, superego, external reality) playing a defensive or compromising role to minimize human conflict; and "superego" as a tyrannical master (father's wrath).[13]

Human creative thought once taught by many religious leaders such as Buddha, Confucius, Jesus, Mohammed and others, and by deep thinkers such as Socrates and Aristotle, had a revival in the eighteenth and nineteenth centuries, when Kant, Kierkegaard and others developed modern phenomenology and existentialism. Their renewed influence in the second half of the twentieth century is seen in the development of humanistic psychology, known as the third force in psychology.[14] Just as Freud introduced human psychic phenomena into the mechanistic model of man--the man of behaviorism--Alfred Adler is known as the important psychologist who disengaged himself from the Freudian model of man and developed an "anthropomorphic" model of man.[15] Adler asserts man's dynamic creative power, unique style of life, purposive behavior, subjectivity, and fictional finalism. He rejects heredity and environment as determining factors in human behavior, but accepts that they are to give "only the frame and the influence which are answered by the individual in regard to his styled creative power."[16]

By the 1950's, an appreciable number of psychologists had become "restive over behaviorism," and were searching for more useful theories that would be both professional and humane.[17] A few to be mentioned at this point are (a) Gordon Allport's motivation theory, which denounces human striving for equilibrium, tension reduction, as well as the death wish, but asserts human intention of behavior; (b) Herbert Bonner's theory of pro-action, which denounces the paradigms of scientism

4

orientation, but asserts the transcending power of human nature; (c) Abraham Maslow's theory of self-actualization, which suggests "peak-experience" as the human potentiality; and (d) Carl Rogers' theory of self, which emphasizes the goodness of human nature as forward moving, constructive, realistic, and trustworthy--not as fundamentally hostile, anti-social, destructive, or a helpless tabula rasa.

Another development in psychology during the 1960's would be transpersonal psychology, the fourth force in psychology.[18] There appears, however, to be very little difference between humanistic psychology and transpersonal psychology in relation to their conceptualization of man and philosophical premises. Sutich describes the nature of transpersonal psychology as follows:

> Transpersonal psychology is concerned specifically with the scientific study and responsible implementation of becoming, individual and species-wide meta-needs, ultimate values, unitive consciousness, peak experiences, B-values, ecstasy, mystical experience, awe, being, self-actualization, essence, bliss, wonder, ultimate meaning, transcendence of the self, spirit, oneness, cosmic awareness, individual and species-wide synergy, maximum interpersonal encounter, sacralization of everyday life, transcendental phenomena, cosmic self-humor and playfulness, maximum sensory awareness, responsiveness and expression, and related concepts, experiences and activities.[19]

Fall of Scientism, and Rise of Humanism

In a Socratic dialogue between Albert Einstein and James Murphy, Einstein says, "I can think of nothing more objectionable than the ideal of science for the scientist. It is almost as bad as art for the artists and religion for the priests."[20] And, also, in a dialogue between Planck and Murphy, we read that science cannot solve the ultimate mystery of nature, including human nature. Such mystery of nature is only to be approximately described by the service of science--not the object of scientific control.

Unfortunately, the Lockean tradition has contributed to the development of scientism, which has asserted abstraction and randomness of human existence via animal existence. Within the framework of such assertion, knowledge built inductively should be based on the accepted facts, but has to operate with "no-verification-but-assumption," which implies that facts once accepted are always to remain the same in the universal phenomena. To build knowledge deductively implies that one should have a concept which is to be unconditionally accepted as the absolute foundation from which the deduction proceeds. The problem, however, is whether there is an absolute concept--whatever that is--since there is no assurance that "what is absolute in science today will remain absolute for all time."[21] Then, when one fails to justify the absoluteness of the concept (construct validity), or when his absolute is removed or disqualified, his knowledge falls to the ground.[22] Therefore, permanence of an "absolute" only exists beyond scientific paradigms, and accordingly is unreachable by scientific researchers. Over and over again, in the history of science, it has happened that a concept that once was looked upon as the absolute is subsequently shown to be merely of relative value, i.e., Darwin's theory of evolution, and Newtonian physics (gravity theory) replaced by Einstein's relativity theory.

Burglar theory--"the theory of the burglar" in Michael Polanyi's term--upon which science heavily relies, appears to be so inferior that a simple poetic truth in human works of fiction cannot be readily proved by the scientists.[23] Man experienced every intuitive creativity before he attempted the scientific study of nature. Therefore, as Polanyi contends, "Science is the late child of the Renaissance."[24] The scientific facts verified in the space age are consonant with King David's appreciation of the beauty of the universe as revealed in his Psalms. Thus, it appears to be appropriate to regard discovery in natural science as guided not so much by the potentiality of a scientific assumption, but by the mysterious operation of human minds.

"Law of Causation" certainly is a major scientific formula used to describe universal phenomena. "Cause-and-effect" has become general knowledge in human life--a common sense that all events and things are the products of other events and things called "cause."[25] This fundamental principle of causation simply implies that from the same or similar sensory complexes as cause, the same or similar sensory complexes will follow as an effect. The assumption which the cause-effect paradigm heavily relies on is that our conduct in everyday life is regulated.

Contrary to scientific assumptions and the cause-effect paradigm, the human being has a more direct and intimate source of knowledge, which is the human consciousness telling man that

6

in the last resort his thought and volition are not subject to simple cause-effect consequences. Uniquely possessing "self-indication" (George Herbert Mead's notion) or "fictional finalism" (Alfred Adler's notion), the inner voice of human consciousness assures that at any given moment the human being is capable of willing this or that alternative. As vonBertalanffy concludes, the characteristic of modern science, the scheme of isolable units, has been proved to be insufficient; and therefore, to conceive human behavior and society properly, we should take into account what "variously and loosely" is called adaptiveness, purposiveness, goal-seeking and the like.[26] Furthermore, the cause-effect paradigm is deprived of all deeper meaning, and also falls short of furnishing us with the grounds of any concrete knowledge. Simultaneously, other scientific paradigms, such as parsimony (complex to simple), reductionism, plenitude, extrapolation, determinism, homeostasis and so on, are being faced with serious questions [27] due to their inability to describe human phenomena.

Thus, in the twentieth century, a truly significant development is the rebirth of science (Renaissance of Science)--the proclamation of scientists to identify their disciplines with humanism. In the school of behaviorism, W. F. Day claims that behaviorism is humanism because it endeavors to understand human behavior to solve problems.[28] K. MacCorquodale, in his article "Behaviorism is a Humanism," describes science for freeing humanity, and emphasizes:

> When science discovers the variables that control man's behavior, man does not lose his autonomy and freedom; at worst, he discovers that they had unsuspected limits...the limits are those imposed by the law of nature.[29]

Elsewhere, the well known behaviorist B. F. Skinner defines "control" as for the benefit of the controllee, and further claims for behaviorism not only the simple term "humanism" but also the distinction of being "effective humanism." "It is because," he continues, "it deeply is concerned with the problems facing us in the world today, and sees a chance to bring the methods of science to bear on these problems, and is fully aware of the dangers of the misuse of the power they are creating."[30]

M. Markovic writes of Marxism as humanism. According to Markovic, Marxism has a "democratic character" standing against such human conditions as "the privatization of individual,

7

class, national, and racial egosim, one-sided obsession with technology, material possessions, political power," which all contribute to degradation of man, to destructive instincts, and to emptiness and meaninglessness of human existence.[31] The term "humanism" also is employed by several socialistic philosophers to justify the democratization of their communist societies.[32]

Atheism, as well as its opposites such as Catholicism, Judaism and Protestantism, all equally declare their "ism" which breed humanism.[33] H. J. Eysenck at the London University Institute of Psychiatry, defines humanism as a combination of reason and compassion; and especially Kurtz endeavors to define humanism with a heavier emphasis on human reason, human potentiality, equal right and human participation, and further contributes to the development of a theory of human liberation, emancipation of man, and enhancement of individual human experience.[34] Along with these atheistic humanists, Christians join the crusade of humanism, proclaiming that Christianity is humanism.[35] In Pope Paul VI's Christmas message of 1969, he indicated that Roman Catholicism was a form of Christian Humanism which not only includes Christ but also advocates "greater justice, wider brotherhood, and a more humane ordering of social relationships."[36]

As we shall read in later paragraphs in this chapter as well as in following chapters, humanistic psychology is a discipline rooted in the spirit of Christianity. The forerunners of humanistic psychology all equally had a fertile soil of Christian spirit; Bonner grew up in Catholicism and practiced Christian morality; Maslow claims a Judeo-Christian orientation; Rogers is a Protestant, once a student at Union Theological Seminary. They, as well as their surviving colleagues such as Bugental and Progoff, call their scientific discipline "humanistic" psychology, "the Renaissance in Psychology."[37]

Sociology also appears to be in a painful labor to give "radical sociology" -- or humanistic sociology--birth into the academic community. As we read, J. F. Glass indicates that unlike traditional sociology which "focuses on man's adjustment to society, on conformity and adaptation, on man as a controlled product of society and culture," humanistic sociology focuses on "man as a determiner of his own fate."[38]

Thus, many behaviorists and humanistic psychologists, as well as Marxist economists, and even some atheists proclaim humanism as their primary "ism" so that the term <u>humanity</u> or <u>humanism</u> has become an honorable badge for twentieth century man.

Definition of Humanism

Humanism is a fellowship of human individuals united by faith, love, hope, and also a "personal" belief in man, "man-of-who" or "whomanism," not "man-of-what"; man of Humanum (natural superiority) and man of Faith (supernatural quality).[39]

Martin Buber writes that an authentic believing humanism is a combination of two qualities in the life of persons--the true knowledge of Humanum and the exercise of Faith: "the natural humanity in which man is at home and which he needs only unfold, cultivate," and a detachment from the human, in which "as it were, he raises himself toward God."[40] Buber sees these two qualities as separate spheres in human life, yet "so centrally related to each other that we may say our faith has our humanity as its foundation, and our humanity has our faith as its foundation."[41]

These two fundamental qualities of man simultaneously become the rational foundation, as Heidegger asserts, of "who is man?" rather than "what is man?" as we study the nature of man. Is man, then, piled up, arranged, or built with different physiological parts which perform various functions in accordance with their expectation? Is man equally a living creature inside of which the constitution of biological metabolism is observed as identical to other creatures? Is man really a union of the atoms in a molecule? In short, is man really a mere structure?

To conceptualize man through the conventional scientific methods, we should organize an assumption of man as "structure." Structure is synonymous with constitution, rooted in Latin "structra," "structus" which implies "put together" or "arrangement of particles." Freud used a topographical structure, and the mechanical and behavioristic view of man endeavors to postulate man as nothing but an ordinal moving organism operating on the basis of "input-output" paradigm, or "C.P.A." (consequence, process, antecedence) paradigm, all of which are recognized as having utility in describing universal phenomena scientifically.[42]

9

In addition to behavioristic and psychoanalytic views of man, A.J. Heschel presents several definitions of man, such as Watson LaBarre's "heat-producing metabolism"; Aristotle's man as "rational animal"; Plato's zoomorphic view of man as "tow legged animal without feathers"; Benjamin Franklin's man as "homo faber, a tool making animal"; pre-Nazi Germany's "bio-chemical component of human body" (which "contains a sufficient amount of fat to make seven cakes of soap, enough iron to make a medium-sized nail, a sufficient amount of phosphorus to equip two thousand match-heads, enough sulphur to rid one's self of one's fleas"); and man as defined by the Encyclopedia Britannica (11th edition)--"a seeker after the greatest degree of comfort for the least necessary expenditure of energy."[43]

In conclusion, Heschel denounces these views simply because these are underestimating of man and further relinquish human self. Knowledge of man is built not with "animality" which is zoologically describable and classifiable, but with "humanity" which seeks for an authenticity of essence and genuineness. "Ignorance about man is not lack of knowledge but false knowledge."[44]

The precariousness of being human, according to Heschel, is that on one hand, man is hard of inner hearing; has sharp and avid eyes; has power to unlock; has capacity for extravagance, sumptuousness, presumption; has exclusive power; is boundless, is resistant to temptation; and has strength in facing frustration. On the other hand, man can be stiff-necked, callous, cruel, refusing to open himself, to hear, to see, and to receive. In other words, man swings to and fro like a pendulum, and accordingly "man is but a short, critical stage between the animal and the spiritual."[45]

Heschel's major theme is to suggest that when we endeavor to understand man, we should look into the image of man rather than the structure of man. This because, as Maurice Stanley Friedman suggests, the image of man retains the wholeness of the person--not displacing the center of man's existence from the person.[46] The word "image" -- "imagin," "imago" -- implies "a reproduction of a person or thing," not only structurally but also symbolically, retaining the identical value of the original. "Image" in other words means "incarnation," which implies a potential structural change but containing the identical inner value. For example, an individual's structural body may be dead but his uniquely possessed values remain the same. Christ, for example, is the incarnated God, transformed

10

into human being, but possessing the same spiritual values as God.

We must, therefore, ask ourselves what the image of man is, what man is after, and where man is from. Whose image is that which man possesses by incarnation? The Bible presents man as created in the image of God:

> And God made the beast of the earth after his kind, and cattle after their kind, and everything that creepeth upon the earth after his kind: and God saw that it was good.
> And God said, Let us make man in our image, after our likeness: and let them have dominion over the fish of the sea, and over the fowl of the air, and over the cattle, and over all the earth, and over every creeping thing that creepeth upon the earth.
> So God created man in his own image, in the image of God created he him; male and female created he them. (Gen.1:25-27) [47]

Social Work and Views of Man

During the Progressive Era (1896-1916), the "preorganized social work era," the prevailing ideas (although they were varied, contrasting and conflicting) were discernable in the public mind. They were Sumner-Darwinism and "mind-your-own-business philosophy" which resulted in ideas of industrial competition, self-responsibility, economic individualism, and further inequality in wealth and income, a prevailing sanction of individual competition, [48] and a belief in charity as a domain of individual relationship.

As Edward T. Devine indicates, however, there were many social work leaders during this era such as Josephine Shaw Lowell, O.T. Bannard, R.W. deForest, A.B. Jennings, and Charles S. Loch from London Charity Organization Society—who are named as the persons responsible for initiating organized social work practice such as children's aid societies, charity organization societies, state boards of charity, the National Conference of Charities and Correction, professional social work schools and social work journals, as well as many other protective and reform programs. And further, they developed social ideologies which proposed that poverty was a "social evil," and that its eradication was a social responsibility.

In general, social workers in the Progressive Era were called "social doctors who practiced social quackeries," but

11

despite such critics they fought against the idea of good "haves" and bad "have-nots" and against the idea of individual inferiority of the Poor.[49] In the 1920's however, psychoanalytic theory came into the theoretical foundation of the social work profession, so that social workers connected their professional activities with psychiatry. Such "pessimistic, non-religious and highly sexual" theory--particularly a theory based on the concept of childhood sexuality--unfortunately resulted in emphasizing human sexual behavior and unconsciousness, neglecting the more rational cognitive process of mind.[50] Yet the idea of humanization has never disappeared from professional social work.

"Do not despise a single human being," wrote Mary Richmond. "He is made of" she continues, "the same materials as mankind in general . . . Caseworkers must not forget that there can be neither discovery nor advance without a spirit of devotion to the human element in which they are working."[51] Therefore, she further emphasized the fullest possible participation of the client, and directed action of mind on mind, and the spirit of freedom to grow through experience.

Currently, Helen Perlman states that "it is necessary to know what he (client) wants for himself in the future, what his aspirations or conceptions of becoming are." And she further emphasized that "within the limits of reality, each man has the right to be master of his soul and of his fate."[52] Henry Miller advocates social work policy which is developed on the basis of human value and dignity--the policy which recognizes individuality, human creativity and responsibility--and further accepts the fact that man is a creature of dignity and that he is entitled to infinite respect simply by the virtue of the fact that he is a man.[53]

Gordon Hearn says that "to promote growth, the social worker relies more upon environmental manipulation and the development of insight and capacity in people than upon methods of imposition."[54] And for William E. Gordon, "Assuring the maximum realization of every individual's human potentiality is becoming a universal societal goal. Social work may find that giving each person a chance to grow and develop in his human aspect, to the maximum of his potentials, is the ultimate way to express respect for human dignity."[55] To approximate human potentiality, Miller and Reissman oppose the segment of the antipoverty movement that stresses changing the poor to fit institutions rather than changing institutions to involve the poor. They suggest that it is necessary to change institutions to fit people by utilizing the positives in the tradition, style, culture, and ways of the poor as one crucial lever in bringing about the needed structural change.[56]

Frankel suggests "transformed or enlarged social work practice," including a concept which calls attention to human social needs, not emphasizing individual change as the necessary concept, but social environment change because of structural deficiency in the environment. He further asserts his suggestion by saying, "No definite human beings are accountable--only society, only the system."[57] It follows, then, that the prime concern and accountability of professional social work is man, and beside him everything is secondary.

Purpose and Procedure

Humbly joining in the crusade for professional humanization, this study seeks to conceptualize "the man--image of man" -- whom we serve through our professional social work activities, and further to suggest the potential utility of a developed concept of man in professional disciplines and activities for human services. The purpose of this study, however, never implies or promises the development of a "new" philosophy about man for our professional growth, but hopes to integrate some of the concepts regarding man from various schools of thought--theology, humanistic existentialism, and humanistic psychology--into a "humanistic concept of man." This study is by no means intended to challenge the behavioristic and psychoanalytic concepts of man, but rather to supplement them with some humanistic ones, that may eventually yield a clear understanding and a more complete concept of man. Further, it is hoped that the study might encourage and stimulate humanistic ideas which will be useful in professional social work activities and hopefully in other disciplines as well. Additionally, this study advocates the restoration movement of humanity by salvaging the lost human identity drained away or lost "by habit, by wrong cultural attitudes, by traumatic episodes, by erroneous education," and by misleading scientific knowledge which overemphasizes the dichotomy and polarity of human nature.[58] Finally, it is hoped that this study will contribute to developing a "better philosophy" for the social work profession since social work admittedly needs such philosophy.[59]

This study deals primarily with three schools of thought: theology, humanistic existentialism, and humanistic psychology. The King James Bible is selected as the basic and major resource

13

of the study not only because of confusion arising from the writings of numerous theologians of various Christian denominations, but also because "the Bible has given the world a new vision of man," and also because the Bible is not a book about God but a book about man.[60] Additionally, the Bible is selected as the basic source of the study, for the Bible is a message for man, its central purpose is to describe man as being created by God but fallen into sin by his rebellion, and it describes a way of salvation for man.[61]

This study will further be indebted to the existential philosopher Soren Kierkegaard, known as the father of existentialism, and his followers such as Heidegger, Sartre and Buber, all known as Judeo-Christian philosophers who believe in super human power as well as human supernaturality.[62]

Another intellectual descendant of Kierkegaard--Paul Tillich, a Lutheran theologian from Europe, has greatly influenced contemporary American thought, not only in Protestant religion but in societal ideologies in general, especially with his "dialectic" humanism--humanism as a combination of "theology and philosophy," faith and reasoning, or "the negation of the negation," which follows a Hegelian dialectic triad.[63] Tillich's doctrine of man based on existential philosophy and theology will be employed in this study to make connection between theology and humanistic existentialism.

Existence, rooted in the Latin word "existere" meaning literally "to stand out, emerge," involves centering upon the existing person and emphasizes the ontological human being, Dasein, as he is emerging or becoming. Existentialism teaches that there is no such thing as truth or reality for a living human being except as he participates in it, is conscious of it, has some relationship to it. The truth is genuinely experienced on all levels of being, including what is called sub-conscious and unconscious but never excluding the element of conscious decision and responsibility. Furthermore, it claims that no one can ever explain or understand any living human being on the basis of conditioning, formulation of drives, study of discrete mechanism and so on. The more absolutely and completely we formulate the force or drives, the more we are talking about abstractions and not the living human being; mechanism has meaning in terms of person only, not vice versa.

Existentialism, like phenomenology, emphasizes the reality of the immediate human experience in the present moment, and stresses the ultimate aloneness of the individual to work out further the concepts of decision, of responsibility, of choice, of self creation, of autonomy, of identity itself. It characteristically makes more problematic and more fascinating the mystery of lonely self-communication via intuition and empathy, love and altruism, identification with others, and harmony in general.

Leading humanistic psychologists appear to have this same soil of phenomenology and existentialism, and also have their academic ancestors such as Hume, James and Mead. Hume's theory of human mind deals with "quality" of mind--mind as the breeding ground of passion. Four qualities of human mind that Hume enumerates are: (a) "sympathy," which implies human communication of sentiments and passion; (b) "comparison," which implies human capability of judgment and comparing; (c) "pride" or self-applause, which implies self-pleasing independence, subjectivity ("disagreeable with others, but always agreeable to himself"); and (d) "goodness," or generosity of man, which implies human being born with love, generosity, humanity, compassion, gratitude, friendship and so on.[64]

In the late nineteenth century, William James expanded Hume's theory of human mind, and concluded that mind is a "theatre of simultaneous possibility and the absolute unlikeliness of the operation."[65] James's self theory is the source of Rogers's self theory, and symbolic interaction theory in the twentieth century. He discusses the constituents of the human self as (a) empirical self ("me") which includes material self, social self and spiritual self; and (b) pure-ego ("I"), which is the sense of personal identity which does not exist as a fact but as a feeling.[66]

Being influenced by James, George Herbert Mead developed a theory of human self as combination of "I" and "me" but essentially a social structure rising out of social experience. According to Mead, "I" is to respond to a social situation, is within the experience of the individual, gives the sense of freedom of initiative, is not calculable, and is understandable only in terms of right. On the contrary, "me" is a definite organization of the community, is within the world, is an act of moral necessity, and is to be described in terms of duty. Mead's notion of human mind is that mind is "the reflective intelligence" which operates in the presence of the future, and that is constituted of various potentialities of response. He contends that human mind is a social product as well as a producer of phenomena including the creation of new symbols.

15

Symbolic interactionists basically take Mead's notion of "me", while Rogerians take Mead's notion of self,"I". Especially, Carl Rogers combines Mead's self with phenomenology (D. Snygg and A.W. Comb) and develops a client-centered therapy, a non-directive approach, and further supplements T-Group (training group) theory.

Such followers of the Leibnitzian school as Maslow and Bonner are most helpful to this study (due to a personal reason), and their significant works will be reviewed solely in light of their theoretical conceptualization of man, since they are advocates of humanistic psychology whose basic postulates are: (a) man as being more than the sum of organic parts; (b) man as being in a human context which implies "umwelt, mitwelt and eigenwelt"; (c) man of awareness[67] being conscious; (d) man as chooser; and (e) man of intention.

Five essences of man will be discussed in the chapters to follow: the dignity of man, the creativity of man, the freedom of man, the morality of man, and proaction of man.

FOOTNOTES

1. John F. Glass, "The humanistic Challenge to Sociology," Journal of Humanistic Psychology 11 (Fall 1971): 172.

2. C. West Churchman, The Systems Approach (New York, 1968), pp.3-4.

3. The quotation is from Gordon W. Allport, "Scientific Models and Human Morals," Psychological Review 54 (July 1947): 182.

4. See E. B. Schachtel, "On Creative Experience," Journal of Humanistic Psychology 11 (Spring 1971): 26.

5. See, for example, Charles T. Tart and James L. Creighton, "The Bridge Mountain Community: An Evolving Pattern for Human Growth," Journal of Humanistic Psychology 6 (Spring 1966): 55-67; and also E. J. LeShan, Mates and Room Mates: New Styles in Young Marriage (Public Affairs' Pamphlet, 381 Park Ave., New York 10016), No. 468.

6. See Allen Overstreet, Our Free Minds (New York 1941), pp.7-16

7. Gordon Allport, Becoming (New Haven 1966), pp. 7-16

8. Sigmund Koch, "Image of Man Implicit in Encounter Group Theory," Journal of Humanistic Psychology 11 (Fall 1971): 110-111.

9. B. F. Skinner, "The Problem of Control," in Being, Becoming and Behavior, ed. Floyd W. Matson (New York,1967), p.113.

10. Noel Mailloux, "Modern Psychology and Moral Value," in The Nature of Man in Theological and Psychological Perspective, ed. Simon Doniger (New York, 1962), p. 92.

11. Ibid.

12. Gene F. Nameche, "Two Pictures of Man," Journal of Humanistic Psychology 1 (Spring 1961): 76.

13. Ibid.

14. See James F. T. Bugental, "The Third Force in Psychology," Journal of Humanistic Psychology 4 (Spring 1964): 19-26.

15. Heinz L. Ansbacher, "Alfred Adler and Humanistic Psychology," Journal of Humanistic Psychology 11 (Spring 1971): 55.

16. Ibid.

17. The quotation is from Koch, "Image of Man," 111

18. Anthony J. Sutich, "Transpersonal Psychology: An Emerging Force," Journal of Humanistic Psychology 8 (Spring 1968): 77-78.

19. Abraham Maslow was the originator of the third force in psychology, and simultaneously acted as an advocate for the fourth force. See Koch, "Image of Man," and Sutich, "Transpersonal Psychology," 77.

20. See Max Karl Ludwig Planck, Where is Science Going (New York 1932), pp. 209-217.

21. Ibid., p. 11.

22. As an example, Planck discusses Avogodros's Law which has a relative connotation as well as a certain absolute significance. (Where is Science Going, p. 173.)

23. See Michael Polanyi, Science, Faith and Society (London, 1964), pp. 8-9. By "the theory of the burglar," Polanyi means, ". . .--which represents our discovery--does not involve any definite relation of observational data from which further new observations can be definitely predicted. It is consistent with an infinite number of possible future observations."

24. Ibid., p. 11.

25. See Planck, Where is Science Going, p. 117: "A regular interrelation between effects that follow one another in time is a cause."

26. Ludwig vonBertalanffy, "General Systems Theory," General Systems 1(1956): 6.

27. Polanyi, for example, questions the rationality of simplicity. See Polanyi, Science, Faith and Society, p. 16.

28. William F. Day, "Humanistic Psychology and Contemporary Behaviorism," The Humanist 31 (Mar./Apr.1971): 13-16.

29. Kenneth MacCorquodale, "Behaviorism is a Humanism." The Humanist 31 (Mar./Apr. 1971): 12-13.

30. B. F. Skinner, "Utopia and Human Behavior," The Humanist 27 (July/Aug. 1967): 120-126; idem., "Humanistic Behaviorism," ibid., 31 (May/June 1971): 35.

31. Mihailo Markovic, "The Basic Characteristics of Marxist Humanism," The Humanist 29 (Jan./Feb.1969): 19-23.

32. See, for example, Paul Kurtz, et al., "Definition of Humanism," The Humanist 31 (July/Aug. 1971): 4.

33. Atheism is referred to as a philosophy, disbelieving the existence of God, but believing in revelation of human reason.

34. See H. J. Eysenck, "Reason with Compassion," The Humanist 31 (Mar./Apr. 1971): 25, where he defines humanism as "the use of reason in human affairs, applied in the service of compassion." See also Paul Kurtz, "Humanism and the Freedom of the individual," The Humanist 29 (Jan./Feb. 1969): 14-19; idem., "The Moral Revolution: Toward a Critical Radicalism," ibid., 31 (Mar./Apr. 1971): 4-5; idem., "Definition of Humanism," ibid., 31 (July/Aug.1971): 4-5.

35. Christian humanism is referred to as a philosophy believing in the existence of God, and his deity, and therefore, includes Catholicism, Judaism and Protestantism.

36. V. Miano, "Meaning and Limits of a Christian Humanism," The Humanist 31 (May/June 1971): 32.

37. I. Progoff, "Toward a Depth Humanistic Psychology," Journal of Humanistic Psychology 10 (Fall 1970): 125.

38. See Glass, "The Humanistic Challenge," 170-183.

39. Called "personal" because every individual has the right to define humanism as he feels. "Whomanism" is suggested by Dr. Raymond W. Swan as synonymous with "man-of-who." Dr. Swan is associate professor of social work at Tulane University school of Social Work, New Orleans, Louisiana.

40. Martin Buber, A Believing Humanism: My Testament, 1902-1965 (New York, 1967), pp. 117-121.

41. Ibid., p. 117.

42. L. R. Goulet and Paul B. Baltes, ed., Life-Span Developmental Psychology (New York, 1970). Goulet and Baltes and their associates initiate what is called developmental psychology, and their recent book (1970) deals with several mathematical research methodologies especially contributing to studies on aging. C. P. A. is one of the paradigms.

43. Abraham J. Heschel, Who is Man (Stanford, 1966), pp. 20-31.

44. Ibid., p. 6.

45. Ibid., pp. 99-103.

46. See Maurice Stanley Friedman, "Existential Psychotherapy and the Image of man," Journal of Humanistic Psychology 4 (Fall 1964): 104-117.

47. Chapters II, III, IV and V deal with further discussion on the image of God in terms of dignity, creativity, freedom, and morality.

48. See Edward Thomas Devine, When Social Work Was Young (New York, 1939).

49. See, for example, William G. Sumner, What Social Classes Owe to Each Other (New York, 1883). Sumner was a major critic of social reform.

50. Herman Borenzweig, "Social Work and Psychiatric Theory: A Historical Analysis," Social Work 16 (Jan. 1971): 7-16.

51. Mary E. Richmond, What is Social Casework (New York, 1925), p. 126.

52. Helen H. Perlman, Social Casework (Chicago, 1964), pp. 6, 60.

53. Henry Miller, "Value Dilemma in Social Casework," Social Work 13 (Jan. 1968): 27-35.

54. Gordon Hearn, *Theory Building in Social Work* (Toronto, 1958),

p. 36.

55. William E. Gordon, "Basic Constructs for an Integrative and Generative Conception of Social Work," *The General Systems Approach*, ed. Gordon Hearn (New York, 1969), p. 5.

56. Seymour M. Miller and Frank Reissman, *Social Class and Social Policy* (New York, 1968), pp. 52-64.

57. See Charles Frankel, "The Moral Framework of the Idea of Welfare," in *Welfare and Wisdom*, ed. John Smith Morgan (Toronto, 1966), pp. 147-164; idem., "Transformation of Welfare," ibid., pp. 165-184. See also Frankel, *The Democratic Prospect* (New York, 1962), p. 147.

58. The quotation is from Abraham H. Maslow, *Toward a Psychology of Being* (New York, 1968), p. 164.

59. Walter L. Kindelsperger, "An Inquiry into the Anatomy of Social Work Knowledge," in Tulane University School of Social Work, *Modes of Professional Education* (New Orleans, 1969), pp. 170-196.

60. Heschel, *Who is Man*, p. 119.

61. J. I. McCord, "Know Thyself: The Biblical Doctrine of Human Depravity," in *The Nature of Man*, ed. Doniger, p. 23.

62. Heidegger is known as a existential philosopher although he was a psychiatrist by profession.

63. See Leonard F. Wheat, *Paul Tillich's Dialectical Humanism: Unmasking the God Above God* (Baltimore, 1970), pp. 77, 234.

64. David Hume, *Treatise of Human Nature* (Oxford, 1739), pp. 592-605.

65. William James, *The Principles of Psychology* (New York, 1890), p. 288.

66. Ibid., p. 329.

67. See Bugental, "The Third Fource," 19-26.

CHAPTER II

THE DIGNITY OF MAN

Definition of Dignity

Dignity implies the quality beyond ordinal ones--the quality of qualities. It is the quality which cannot be measured-- incomparable and atypical, different from and transcending other quality and value. Such quality is only subject to be respected and honored at any and all cost.

Human dignity refers to the quality of man, which in the absolute differs from that of any other creature in the universe, beyond measurement and comparison. It beautifies man and makes humanity noble. Further, it is the intrinsic worth of man, the nature of universal equality in a human being. By simple virtue of being a man, a human being owns dignity.[1]

Soren Kierkegaard believed in "blessed equality of man"--an equality of essential relation to God entering into personal union with Him--and "an equality of freedom to will the good of the human organism, which has a motivation of togetherness in a form of brotherhood and neighborhood--mutuality--built upon God. For Kierkegaard, man is fullness of strength rather than weakness, honest humility rather than self-deception.[2] Moreover, only man is associated with sanctity and dignity, and therefore, intrinsically sacred and supremely valuable, while other creatures in the universe are made holy and sacred by man. Man, as Heschel says, is "precious."[3]

Another documentation of human dignity in the form of absolute difference is made by Heidegger in his term "Dasein"--Da and Sein--meaning "always there." Heidegger employs "Being" (Sein) in an effort of separating man from general beings, "sein or bleiben." He believes that man is a being of superiority and absoluteness, and therefore, Sein is not compared with a sein. "Man-ness" implies Dasein of Being, or man. Thus, Heidegger uses Dasein as synonymous to "man":

> Dasein is an entity which does not just occur among other entities. Rather it is ontically distinguished by the fact that, in its very Being, that Being is an issue for it . . . This is a constitutive state of Dasein's Being, and this implies that Dasein, in its Being, has a relationship toward that Being--a relationship which itself is one of Being . . .

Understanding of Being is itself a definite characteristic of
Dasein's Being.[4]

Heidegger's view of man has history in relation to time
(Zeit): (a) "ontical" nature, which is a historical property of
man--the determinate character of existence; (b) ontological
nature, which is man's property in his present existence; and
(c) ontic-ontological nature, which is a property and a
possibility for his future existence. Existentialism, however,
believing in Dasein's ontical nature, emphasizes ontological and
ontic- ontological natures of Dasein. The nature of Dasein
should be everything, everywhere and every time--"being here and
being there," always.[5] It follows from Heidegger that man is
not one of the objects in the world--one of "be's or being," but
he is what himself is, he is in him, him is in he--the combined
Being.

"Togetherness" of man implies man understanding himself in
terms of ontological Being, being-with-others,
being-in-the-world. One more step further; it implies
"being-with-beings." Therefore, his being-with/in-himself does
not necessarily mean his being isolated from others, but rather
being-with/in-others, because of his ontical nature and because,
through beings, he can approximate the meaning of his present
existence.

Being-with-others further implies "Sorge"--concern, care,
interpreted sometimes as a "a priori." This is an essence of
existential mutuality, "you-and-I" without which there would be
no Being. "Empathy does not first constitute Being-with, only
on the basis of Being-with does empathy become possible." Thus,
Heidegger uses the word being-in-the-world as the essential
state of Dasein because being-in-the-world belongs essentially
to Dasein. Dasein, the man, is with many beings, environmental
objects and systems, yet stands out by himself.

Zu-sein implies the potentiality of man in the
future--moving toward his own most possibility in uncertainity.
Practicing his unique and supernatural power of man,
"transcendence," he is capable of overcoming the hardships of
the present and of further enhancing them into his
"perfection"--transformation into that which he can be in Being.
Therefore, man can be positively active in out-going and
foregoing, and can take rigorous training, hardship, danger,
until he discovers his Being and unseen, unexisting beings.
This possibility, for Heidegger, is the essence (Wessen) of
man.[6] Thus, man only is capable of taking on more problematic

situations, and capable of enjoying more fascinating mysteries via his given intuition. Beyond reality, the world of the human mind is opened by human intuition, and further he is willing to pursue the possibility of materializing it in reality. This is the God-given mission to the finite Being, the man.

In contrast to Kierkegaard and Heidegger's notion of human dignity and sanctity, Skinner refers to human dignity as conspicuously manipulatable by man because it is an object of human admiration which is inversely proportional to actuality. Namely, human dignity is extrinsically manipulated "worth" which is primarily undiscovered, hidden content of human behavior. It should mean that the more people are unable to understand the reason why a particular individual behaves in a certain way, the more admiration is to be given to him and the further the amount of his dignity is to be identified. In short, for Skinner, human dignity is the reinforcement for an unknown motivation of individual behavior.

At any rate, man is different from other creatures, from animals and plants, in that he may be respected by virtue of ownership of the highest quality of all. Then, let us ask ourselves how different man's quality is in comparison with the qualities of other creatures.

Human Dignity from the Image of God

In the darkness, disorder, disorganization and nothingness was there the Logos, the Word of God (John 1: 1) who is the One who laid the foundation of the earth and created the universe (Heb. 1: 10). Thus, the Spirit of Creation becomes the Genesis of the existence of the universe.

Upon the completion of the Biblical five-day creation, man was created in the image of God and was crowned as the host of the earth:

So God created man in his own image, in the image of God created he him; male and female created he them.
And God blessed them, and God said unto them, Be fruitful, and multiply, and replenish the earth, and subdue it: and have dominion over the fish of the sea, and over the fowl of the air, and over every living thing that moveth upon the earth (Gen. 1: 27-28).

"Adam was first formed then Eve," (1 Tim. 2: 13) whose name means "life" and who is created from the rib of Adam (not

24

from an animal or not having developed from a process of evolution). She and Adam were created almost simultaneously, and Adam and Eve became one (Gen. 2: 24)--one nature, the beautiful. Edith Dean indicates "the symbolism of Adam's rib" as rib of the Adam's side, nearest to Adam's heart, which symbolizes equal and close relationship of man and woman. Moreover, she portrays Eve as man in femininity, as being elevated to ethereal beauty and lofty dignity, as a great sculptor, a beautiful figure out of Parian marble, as the queen of the universe and fairest of the fair, and as having gleaming golden hair, a lovely face and a strong and immortal form. Man is made in eternal and absolute beauty, thus all man shares the common origin, the offspring of God. This is all what Martin Luther King, Jr. cried out in his speech given at the Kleinhous Music Hall in Buffalo. As a minister, a follower of Gandhi's "Satihagraha," a non-violent minority leader, he wrote a moving poem seeking equality for his people:

> Fleecy looks and Black complexion cannot forfeit
> Nature's claim
> Skins may differ, but affection dwells in
> Black and white the same.
> And I were so tall as to reach the pole or to grasp
> The ocean at a span,
> I must be measured by my soul, the mind is the
> Standard of the man.[16]

All men created after the image of God are beautiful regardless of color, white or black, yellow or red. In the minds of men, it still resounds, "Black is not dirty but beautiful."

According to the Bible, God is invisible and unsearchable:

Behold, I go forward, but he is not there; and backward, but I cannot perceive him: on the left hand, where he does work, but I cannot behold him: He hides Himself on the right hand, that I cannot see Him (Job. 23: 8-9).
The apostles John and Paul also give us messages of the invisibility of God in their writings. John writes, "No man has seen God at any time" (1: 18) and Paul, in his letter to the Colossians and to his spiritual son Timothy, speaks of "the image of the invisible God" (Col. 1: 15) and "the King the invisible" (1 Tim. 1: 17).

The portion we observe, conceive and communicate in man-ness is more or less quantitative, and therefore it is visible and is potential for extrinsic information. Upon such

25

information, we likely build some classifications of average man. In every individual man, however, there is something always which cannot be classified, repeated, duplicated or substituted for normalization and standardization. In other words, each human being lives in a subjective and private world which is absolutely different from the world all human beings share. It is a world of noteworthiness, relevance, and certainty only to the person it belongs to, and further develops into the power of infinite transformation, what Tillich calls "the essence of human nature."[11]

As related to the invisibility of God, God is declared as unsearchable. In the book of Job again, it is written, "Canst thou by searching find out God? Canst thou find out the Almighty unto perfection?" (11: 7) and again, "Touching the almighty, we cannot find him out: he is excellent in power, and in judgment, and in plenty of justice; he will not afflict: (37: 23). Further Biblical references in relation to the unsearchable nature of God are found in Psalm 145: 3--"There is no searching of his praised; and his greatness is unsearchable"; in Isaiah 4: 20--"There is no searching of his understanding"; and in Romans 11: 33--"O the depth of the riches both of the wisdom and knowledge of God. How unsearchable are his judgments."[12]

Many scientists studying human existence have arrived at an agreement that they could search man in the form of machine and in the form of animal behavior. Especially Stanley Hall, who had studied under Wundt in Europe, endeavored to develop a scientific instrument to quantify the qualitative human "essence." Although Hall and his student, such as Thorndike, had a significant influence upon modern scientific technology, their scientific method and measurement instruments are under serious question. One example is whether a standardized I.Q. scoring method based on "normal curve principle" has universal applicability, regardless of time and space. Especially, the validity and reliability of the normal curve principle for measuring human behavior is questioned because of its nature of relativity and situationality, which implies its limitation as a scientific methodology.

Humanistic psychologists wave the banner of "personal world," which is to emphasize consciousness, the function of human mind, and subjective behavior intrinsically valued. But as long as their theoretical conceptualization concludes that the potential operation of human mind is infinite, modern scientific technology falls far short of describing who man is,

26

and therefore man is beyond its reach. As yet, science is far short of describing the "square root of negative numerals," the "concept of zero," or "fourth dimensionality" to which human mind comfortably can expand its operation. To reiterate, the variables of being an individual man are "multi," and cannot be measured or controlled simply because humanity is beyond intellectual and technological structures. Humanity exists in mystery, beyond the reach of any one, anything, but the individual man himself. In this sense, man is wonderful.

Dignity from Righteousness and Holiness

According to the Biblical account, God crowned His creation by forming man, who received the breath of life (Gen. 2: 7, Ps. 33: 6) and become "the image and glory of God" (1 Cor. 11: 7). Furthermore, when man's old nature became corrupted through sin, God provided him with a new nature created after the likeness of God in true righteousness and holiness (Eph. 4: 22-24).

Man is so righteous and holy that God, the Holy Spirit, finds His dwelling place in man. Among many mysteries in the Bible, the mystery of Mary's conceiving (Matt. 1: 18) by the Holy Spirit is the divine testimony of human holiness, and further is the completion of God's promise for the Messiah, the Savior of mankind.

In the New Testament, many important appearances of God himself in man are read, for example, in Acts 1: 8--"Ye shall receive power after that the Holy Ghost is come upon you," where "you" implies man. Elsewhere in the Acts of the Apostles God appears in the form of Holy Spirit in man's behavior. God is righteous and holy, man is His appearance. Thus, L. F. Wheat writes, "Human progress is measureable by the degree to which human beings accept humanity as God and comfort themselves accordingly."[13] As Heschel says, "Life is partnership of God and man."[14]

The most provocatively documented empirical finding is in Carl Rogers's writing. The major theme of Rogers's article "The Nature of Man" is the goodness, trueness, trustworthiness, and dependableness of human nature. Based on his quarter century of professional practice, he arrives at the following conclusions: Man is not fundamentally hostile, antisocial, destructive, evil; man is not a "tabula rasa" whose nature is strictly contingent upon chance without the power of independence; and is not to be a perfect being, but rather sadly warped and corrupted by society.[15] Man is to be positive, forward moving,

27

constructive, realistic and trustworthy. The nature of man in righteousness and trueness has immense power for survival.

Nothing false survives forever. The true content of the story of Jezebel in the Old Testament is to prove death in the case of an unrighteous and unholy man. Jezebel, by being married to King Ahab, brought Baal, the great nature-god, to Israel along with no less than 450 Baal worshipers. But her unrighteous and untruthful behavior in plotting against God ended in nothing but corruption, dissention and death--not only her death but also that of her sons. The wicked shall perish. This is the eternal law given to righteous man.

From the lesson of Calvary, we learn Christ's teaching about human righteousness and goodness. Even on the Cross, Christ did not condemn people who were crucifying him but asked God to forgive them because they did not know what they were doing (Luke 23: 34). This word on the Cross implies that although man commits murder or theft, he can still be forgiven because he does not know what he is doing. The divine endowment of righteousness and holiness is still his as a gift from God, "Something is worth in every one, even in murderer, thief."[16] It follows that man, though often ignorant, may be imputed by God to be righteous. Tillich calls this "Justitia Originalis" which implies that " man in his pure nature is not only the image of God, he has also the power of communion with God and therefore of righteousness toward other creatures and himself."[17]

Dignity from Humanity

Man is placed "a little lower than the angels" and above all creature (Ps. 8: 5), and thus, man is "fearfully and wonderfully made" (Ps. 139: 14).[18] As R. C. Miller puts it, man is holding "dual citizenship"--one citizenship of this world and another of the kingdom of God.[19] Human divine life is "the negation of the negation" which implies that man disobeyed God (negation) but, as we shall see later, man has power to return to God--a synthesis of God and man.[20] Man is not an animal nor an angel, but does have both natures, "animality" and "angelness"--called "Humanity." Such duality of humanity is truly wonderful.

The duality of man is mysterious and therefore "man alone can speak for all beings," and "human living alone enacts the mystery of drama."[21] Moreover, man reaches to the Almighty by transcending all mysteries--not by goodness but by mercy (Job

22: 2-3; Ps. 16: 2), and establishes union with God. As Tillich writes, the meaning of God is "the constituents of man's intrinsic nature," which is part of human ontological substance.[22]

Martin Buber's well known "I-Thou" paradigm, describes well the "duality of manness"—man as "in-between." His paradigm suggests human relations in four basic forms: (a) man and nature: (b) man and man: (c) man and intelligible forms; and (d) man and eternal Thou. The first three are primarily worldly and independent relations—"I-It," and the last is a dependent but direct relation with Thou, "I-Thou."[23]

"I" of "I-Thou" and "I" of "I-It" are not identical. "I" of "I-It" is bound by others, whereas "I" of "I-Thou" is bound by Grace of Thou, which in turn implies whole being. Buber rather describes "I" of "I-It" as being faced by no Thou, surrounded by a multitude of "contents" with no present but only the past. Such as "I" as man is satisfied with worldly things, and lives in the past without present content. He is nothing but an object which "is not duration, but cessation, suspension, a breaking off and cutting clear and hardening, absence of relation and of present being."[24]

The relation between "I-Thou" is mutual. Love is the vehicle of relationship; especially it is the responsibility of "I".[25] Through the Thou a man becomes "I" and "I-Thou" relationship implies that man can address God in very reality, can say Thou to Him, and can stand face to face with Him.[26] It follows that in this way, through this relationship only, holy communion is possible between God and man.

"I-It" relation consists of things such as events and actions; things entered in the graph of place, events in that of time; things which are measurable, comparable, perceivable, ordered and detached; and further repeatable and verifiable. On the other hand, "I-Thou" relation is beyond measurement, comparison; has continually new appearance but no destiny; and has no duration. This relation is not of external existence but internal in the depth of soul.[27]

Buber further suggests two different words, "individuality and person," in an effort to describe the difference between "I" of "I-Thou" and "I" of "I-It." Individuality is developed from "I-It" relation and makes its appearance by being differentiated from other individualities. On the contrary, a person is created in the relation of "I-Thou" and makes its appearance by entering into relationship with other persons. For Buber, individuality is "dying life," but person is "eternal life." And he concludes that "these are not two kinds of man, but two poles of humanity . . . No man is pure person and no man pure individuality. None is wholly real. Every man lives in the twofolded 'I'." Man, thou art two-in-one. Thou art "between." Thou art wonderfully created, thus. Thou art in "hiearchical spiral."[28]

Abraham Maslow's motivation theory appears to be developed from a Biblical concept of "man in between." His term "motivational progression" refers to "give-and-take" lifelong process between DM_{29} (deficiency motivation) and GM (growth motivation) of man. DM is to gratify the basic needs for health, safety, belongings, love, respect and self-esteem, all of which needs are met by others, outside of the subject, while GM is to actualize the potentialities, capabilities and talents, to fulfill one's mission (or call, fate, destiny or vocation), to know and accept the person's intrinsic nature, and to unceasingly endeavor to achieve unity, integration or synergy within the person.[30]

According to Maslow, animals have only DM, but only man has DM and GM both, which are in mutual necessity. The major theme of "motivation progression" is that man cannot have GM only with an unachieved DM, and vice versa--cannot "pass into one another." To be GM oriented, DM has to be satisfactorily achieved beforehand to accommodate GM, and also DM is in need of input from GM as to particular needs, so that DM is achieved accordingly. Without one, there is not the other. Thus, man is created in two motivations of life, not belonging to "either-or" but to both. Man is between, and therefore is "two-in-one."[31]

Dignity from Sinning

By virtue of the utmost mischief of man (Gen. 3), partaking the forbidden fruit of the tree, man was thrown out of the Garden of Eden, and came to know "good and evil" as God does. "Behold, the man is become as one of us, to know good and evil" (Gen. 3: 22)--one of "us" who knows good and evil. This resulted in the "fall of man" and "the rise of human dilemma and predicament."

The Biblical source of sin is disobedience to God, definite negation of God. The original nature of man includes "freedom but finite" (Gen. 3: 3)--finite with divine limitation of "not to eat the fruit." The divine endowment to man of freedom, however, entails many possibilities, including a possibility of misuse. The epistle to the Romans, for example, read, "Wherefore as by one man sin entered into the world, and death by sin; and so death passed upon all men for that all have sinned." (5: 12) Accordingly, there is not man without sin--"There is not a just man upon earth, that doeth good, and sinneth not"--but all men are shapen in sin (Eccles. 7: 20). "Behold, I was shapen in iniquity: and conceived and born in sin" (Ps. 51: 5) and therefore, all men are under sin (Gal. 3: 22; Rom. 3: 9; 11: 32). Thus, sin became one of the universal natures of man, inevitably connected with the divine endowment of human freedom.

Sin is also equated in the Bible with unbelief, rebellion against God, or egocentric idolatory worship. Man does not worship God who created him, but "god" which man has made, it is self-ordered life--substituting himself for God, who knows good and evil.[32] By this, unfortunately, men rather became stiffnecked (Exod. 32: 9) and rebelled against God (Isa. 1: 2), and finally were disqualified from receiving "the things of the spirit of God . . . . spiritually discerned" (1 Cor. 2: 14).

Thus, sin becomes an essence of human nature, originating in disobedience to, and rebellion against, God. Is there any other creature that was thrown out of the peaceful and beautiful Garden of Eden, due to "once-for-all" misuse of divine endowment? None but one, the man. Man labeled as being "sinful," is distinguished from other creatures, and because of his having sinned, he becomes a "more beloved creature" by God than any other. God bestows His mercy upon man only.

As an essence of human nature, potentiality is a dynamic and powerful urge in man. Namely, the human potentiality to search himself before the mirror of righteousness and to confess his unrighteous behavior is truly another divine endowment. Upon this potential quality, all men are divinely ordered to confess their sins (Prov. 28: 13; Luke 15: 21; 1 John 1: 9), that they may receive divine mercy. Thus, existence of human dignity by virtue of being sinful is another mystery of human beings.

Despite such sinful nature of man, as McCord writes, human sin does not originate from nature but is a by-product of man's creatureliness. He explains, "Sin is not a product of the lowest in man's nature, but a product of the misuse of his highest endowment, his capacity for fellowship with God. It is not indigenous to man's true nature but contrary to it. Hence sinful man is 'de-natured' man."[33] In the same manner, Socrates believed human wrong doing to be "involuntary." The ineradicable nature of human behavior is that man temporarily sophisticates himself into regarding evil as good. And further Socrates was convinced that "wrong-doing is due to miscalculation; but the miscalculation is not one of amount of pleasure, but of values of good."[34]

Dignity from Candidacy for Salvation

Human dignity exists in the human fallible nature. Being man, David the King of Israel, once sinned (2 Sam. 11) by adulterous union with Bath-Sheba, wife of Urish who was one of David's beloved generals. Urish was furtively sent to the frontline and killed, that David might be able to legitimize his marriage to Bath-Sheba. David, however, repented for his sin (Ps. 51) and cried for mercy, cleansing from iniquity, re-creation with truth and holiness, and salvation. Upon his sincere and genuine repentance, God blessed him and Bath-Sheba, giving four children from their marriage, including Solomon, and finally establishing the genealogy of Jesus.

We read of two women in the New Testament who demonstrated repentance and self-correcting behavior, and who further revealed human dignity by repentance. A Samaritan woman (John 4), who met Jesus at the Jacob's well in the city of Sychar, confessed her having no husband although she had had five in total, and went to the village with the news of discovering Christ, the Messiah. Another woman (Luke 7) is portrayed as a sinful woman. She brought an alabaster box of ointment and washed Jesus' feet with tears in deep repentance.

Thus, no other single creature in the universe besides man becomes the object of God's love and mercy. Man is the only creature receiving God's love, although he does not deserve it. As Tillich puts it, the love of God is "accepting the person who is not acceptable,"[35] as prophesied by Isaiah (9: 2-6) and Malachi (3: 1), and completed in God's incarnation into Jesus Christ.

For the son of man is come to save that which was lost (Matt. 18: 11).

For the son of man is not come to destroy men's lives, but to save them (Luke 9: 56).

For God sent not his son into the world to condemn the world, but that the world through him might be saved (John 3: 16).

According to theologian William Hamilton, man deserves condemnation, but salvation is offered to all men.[36] Salvation is the spiritual communication for man by living in "faith," "love" and "hope."

This salvation is that which God established "before the world began" and which God is willing to give all men for the knowledge of the truth. Further, salvation is deliverance from sin, uncleanliness and the devil. It is deliverance from wrath, enemies and eternal death.

Salvation is the manifestation of God's grace, love and mercy, rather than the consequence of human works. Paul writes to the Ephesians of salvation by grace (Eph. 2: 9), writes to Timothy of salvation not according to works but God's own purpose and grace (2 Tim. 1: 9), and also writes to Titus in the same manner (Tit. 2: 11). Most of all, Christ's death on the Cross was to save man from sin (Rom. 5: 8; 1 John 4: 9-10).

Thus, sinful man becomes the only object of divine love, while no other creature is appreciative of His love. By salvation, man can re-establish his relationship with God and finally can restore his lost pure image in sin into the true image, the image of God. Salvation is a divinely given potentiality in human nature, which is not earned but freely bestowed. This quality of human dignity is divine.

SUMMARY

Human dignity is the highest quality, divinely bestowed to man, the quality that is given by the Creator of the universe to man, but to no other creature.

With much emphasis on Biblical references, it is concluded that man is created in the image of God and accordingly all men have the same origin. Man was abundantly blessed and the only creature with whom the Creator of the universe was completely satisfied, and therefore, the last creature in order (Gen. 1).

Human being is so righteous and holy that the Holy Spirit is revealed through man, and man becomes partner with God. He lives with God as well as communicates with God.

Man belongs to the world of other creatures. He has "animality," as well as "angelness." In Tillich's term man has "imago" as well as "similitudo." Man therefore swings like a pendulum between two different worlds, but belongs to neither world. He is "betweenist" called "humanity"--"two-in-one" quality.

By virtue of entailment of human freedom, the divine endowment to man, man made a "once-for-all" mistake by disobeying and rebelling against God. Not to any creature did God make any limitation to behave morally, but to man who was bound to desire morality. Man was not to eat the fruit of the tree in the Garden of Eden. Violating the divine order, only man sinned, while no other creature commits any sin.

Being sinful but created in the image of God, man's quality of repentance and self-correction is inevitable. His righteous and holy nature cry out for redemption, and for this reason man has become the object of God's love and mercy and grace, and God's plan of salvation.

Thus, only man, beyond the reach of other creatures, is created in the image of God, is righteous and holy for partnership with God, and is in the mystery of dual quality, or humanity. Only man also committed sin, but because of such an unfortunate fatal occurrence, God reaches man and man rejoices in holy reunion with God.

Man possesses his dignity in his unexchangeable and unequatable value--divine value; even with the whole universe, no single individual life can be purchased. His life is purchased by divine sacrifice, and therefore his life is obligated to love, faith and hope in Christ. Man is beautifully made from the dust but in the image of God, carrying the breath of life.

1. See, for example, Henry Miller, "Value Dilemma in Social Casework," Social Work 13 (Jan. 1968): 27. He says "It (fundamental tenet of social casework and all social welfare, beautiful conception and article of faith of all social work) holds that man is a creature of dignity and that he is entitled to infinite respect--simply by virtue of the fact that he is a man.... Our business is with dignity."

2. James Daniel Collins, The Mind of Kierkegaard (Chicago, 1953), pp. 180-196.

3. Abraham J. Heschel, Who Is Man (Stanford, 1966), p. 33.

4. Martin Heidegger, Being and Time, trans. J. MacQuarrie and E. Robinson (New York, 1962), p. 32.

5. See, for example R. Powell, "The Late Heidegger's Omission of the Ontic-Ontological Structure of Dasein," in Heidegger and the Path of Thinking, ed., John Sallis (Pittsburg, 1970), pp. 117-126.

6. Heidegger, Being and Time, pp. 114-243.

7. B. F. Skinner, Beyond Freedom and Dignity, (New York, 1971), pp. 44-59.

8. The image of God is interpreted in different words in the following Biblical verse: "The similitude of God" (James 3: 9), "after God is" (Col. 3: 10; Eph. 4: 24), and "has crowned with his glory and honor" (Ps. 8: 5).

9. Edith Dean, ed. All of the Women of the Bible (New York, 1955), p. 4.

10. Martin Luther King, Jr., "The Future of Integration, "The Humanist 28 (Mar./Apr. 1968): 2.

11. Paul Tillich, "Existentialism, Psychotherapy, and the Nature of Man," The Nature of Man in Theological and Psychological Perspective, ed. Simon Doniger (New York, 1962), p. 43.

12. See, for non-Biblical references, Susanne Langer's concept of "discursive symbol," in Philosophy in a New Key

(Cambridge, Mass., 1967), pp. 280-284; George Herbert Mead's concept of "I" in Mind, Self and Society (Chicago, 1934), pp. 135-178; and Kierkegaard's "conative factors" of personal integrity, as interpreted by James Daniel Collins, The Mind of Kierkegaard (Chicago, 1953), p. 156.

13. Leonard F. Wheat, Paul Tillich's Dialectical Humanism: Unmasking the God Above God (Baltimore, 1970), p. 241.

14. Heschel, Who is Man, p. 75.

15. Carl R. Rogers, "The Nature of Man," in The Nature of Man. ed. Doniger, pp. 91-93.

16. Attributed to prison reformer Marthilda Wrede (Finland, 1864-1928), as quoted by H. Winthrop, "Self-Sacrifice as Autonomy, Ego-Transcendence and Social Interest," Journal of Humanistic Psychology 2 (Fall 1962): 31-37.

17. Paul Tillich, Systematic Theology I (Chicago, 1965), p. 258.

18. See Heb. 2: 8, and James 3: 7.

19. R. C. Miller, "Theology and the Understanding of Children," in The Nature of Man, ed. Doniger, p. 144.

20. The quotation is from Wheat, Paul Tillich's Dialectical Humanism, p. 77.

21. Heschel, Who is Man, p. 77.

22. Paul Tillich, Morality and Beyond, vol. 9 (New York, 1963), p. 9.

23. Martin Buber, I and Thou, tran. R. G. Smith (New York, 1953), p. 12.

24. Ibid.

25. Ibid., pp. 14-15.

26. Malcolm Luria Diamond, Martin Buber: Jewish Existentialist (New York, 1960), p. 5.

27 Buber, I and Thou, p. 31-32.

28. Ibid., pp. 62-65. Hierarchical spiral implies "mutual belongness" between the two polarities, and external process of transfiguration of man. Not either-or being, but neither-nor being. A similar term is used by Maslow--"Hierarchically integrated." See Maslow, Toward a Psychology of Being, p. 172.

29. Abraham Maslow, Toward a Psychology of Being, p. 26.

30. Ibid, pp. 22-25. See also pages 24-43 for further comparison.

31. "Two-in-one" nature of man is described by Tillich in his book, Systematic Theology I, p. 258. For Tillich, the image of God implies two meanings, "imago" and "similitudo."

32. See Genesis 2.

33. J. I. McCord, "Know Thyself: The Biblical Doctrine of Human Depravity," in The Nature of Man, ed. Doniger, pp. 23-24.

34. Alfred Edward Taylor. Socrates (New York. 1933), pp. 133-135.

35. Tillich, Morality and Beyond, p. 9.

36. William Hamilton, "A Theology for Modern Man," in The Nature of Man, ed. Doniger, pp. 218-236.

Chapter III

THE CREATIVITY OF MAN

Definition of Creativity

Human activities of discovery are revealed in forms of competition for the minds of men.[1] Historically, it is possible to trace a transition of the "discovering" behavior of man from a religious connotation (creativity as a "divine gift," "some kind of rare, hereditary blessing") to scientific quality.[2] "Who discovers a new thing first?" is a question asked in the name of "creativity." This human creativity has been described as the most important human quality in changing history and in shaping the world and the "most basic manifestation of man's fulfilling his own being in his world."[3]

Who makes a new and better commodity for human life? How does he do it? Who introduces a new and better technology for the advancement of human life? How does he do it? Who produces the best-seller? Again, how does he do it? How can I make my environment better for my life? These are among the seemingly unavoidable questions in the minds of men today. Such human questions become more and more the serious object of science, especially in the fields of education, psychology, and political science. Educators and educational psychologists endeavor to implement psychologists' methodologies solely to facilitate and procure human creativity; clinical psychologists endeavor to define creativity and introduce elaborate methodologies to enhance and enrich human creativity; and politicians endeavor to be instrumental in providing systematic government under which citizens exercise their creativity, and consequently create a new and better government of people, democracy.

Although "it is clear that no single definition has been prepared," this writer will review some literature to arrive at a tentative definition of creativity.[4]

A. Psychological Perspectives on Creativity

Psychologists, in general, define creativity as either "process" or "product." (1) <u>Creativity as Process</u>. Morris I.

Stein defines creativity as a "resultant process" occurring in the individual, or in social transaction, resulting in "novel work" accepted as tenable, useful, or satisfying by a group at some point in time. He also calls creativity "a process of hypothesis testing and the communication of results."[5] Crutchfield discusses "creative process" as one of many individual life processes, which are "a complete set of cognitive and motivational processes in the individual, and processes which are involved in perceiving, remembering, thinking, imagining, deciding"; in other words, "the general cognitive and motivational functioning of the individual."[6]

Guilford delineates "divergent" and "convergent" thinking processes in man. For Guilford, divergent thinking includes a variety of mental and behavioral responses of man as he responds to stimuli--not preprogrammed determination by the given informational input, but rather a pragmatic, trial-and-error approach implying spontaneous flexibility.[7] It means to think differently and to seek some new, optional variety, and is therefore creative. In systems theory it is synonymous with multifinality, progressive segregation or catabolism, which implies arrival at a variety of consequences from an isomorphic origin.

Convergent thinking includes "the drawing of fully determined conclusions from given information." For example, Charles is younger than Robert. Charles is older than Frank. "Who is older, Robert or Frank?" The answer is already implied in the transitive nature of the statements. Thus, convergent thinking is a process of imagining, synthesizing, abstracting and reasoning to produce new insight and new information. At this point, convergent thinking moves into a new process of divergent thinking, and is therefore creative. Convergent thinking is also synonymous with such systems terms as equifinality, progressive systematization or anabolism which implies arrival at an isomorphic consequence from various origins.

Frank Barron defines creativity as "an internal process continually in action but not always observable, or perhaps in some cases fundamentally unobservable," and as something that is happening in the central nervous system. He believes "product" is an accidental consequence of constant and various "trial-and-error" series in the absence of thinking process.[8] Therefore he concludes product is not creativity.

39

Gordon seems to integrate Guilford's concepts of divergent and convergent thinking and Barron's notion of creativity as mental activity, and suggests the term "synectics," which defines creative process as the mental activity in problem-solving situations where artistic or technical inventions are the result. He further describes a synectic process as two major mental processes: (a) process making the strange familiar, which involves understanding, analyzing, concretely assuming, comparing, and consequently converting the strangeness into familiarity; and (b) process making the familiar strange, which involves distorting, inverting, transposing familiar everyday ways as though they are momentarily strangers, and consequently developing new ideas by seeing the same thing differently.[9]

Thus, according to a definition of creativity as process, creative product is a consequence of creative process which precedes the products, or is an accidental consequence of simple trial-and-error. Intellectual ability and new ideas are products of creative process, and some chemical products represent products of trial-and-error, the consequences of series of combinations of chemical elements.

(2) Creativity as Product. Without an objectified product, creativity remains only abstract and elusive. Whatever the mental processes—either divergent or convergent—they may extend the potential boundaries of the creativity (product), but may not increase the quantity and quality of the product. Furthermore, the processes are the necessary basis for creative productivity, but are necessarily "creativity."

New or modified products in the perceptual world are not only the measure of, but the true meaning of, creativity. Rollo May suggest creativity as "the process bringing something new into birth," namely, the primary measure of creativity is on the basis of the product which is resultant process—or achievements in the epiphenomena, to use Abraham Maslow's term.[10] Carl Rogers also suggests creative process as "the emergence in action of a novel relational product, growing out of the uniqueness of the individual on the one hand, and the materials, events, people, or circumstance of his life on the other"—as a product of combination of the individual product and environmental products.[11]

Another view of creativity as product is described by Harold H. Anderson.[12] In addition to his description of creativity as being associated with "a painting, a sculpture, a

40

sonnet, and invention, a product that can be seen, studied, enjoyed," he describes creativity as a "psychological or social invention, whose product is not an object as such," yet in "novelty"--not an observable product, but a product in an individual's mind in relation to his environment.[13] Such creativity in human relations is revealed in two systems: (a) social and political systems, i.e., "Magna Charta, the Bill of Rights, the Emancipation Proclamation, constitutions, bylaws and their amendments, codes of law, and city ordinances"; and (b) cultural systems, i.e., "arranging car pools, keeping on good terms with one's neighbors, courting, making love, and child rearing.

(3) Other Views of Creativity. There seem to be many other psychological views on creativity. Among them are Sigmund Freud and K. Abraham's notion of creativity as a resultant sublimation.[14] There is also a notion of "individual reaction to heredity and environment in a socially affirmative fashion" --courageous and communal intuition.[15] Leonard Steinberg and Eric Fromm suggest that creativity is a character trait. Steinberg writes: "Creativity may be defined as a characteristic with which a person is born; a talent, a unique capacity, an aptitude. And it is a phenomenon conditioned by certain social and economic circumstances which foster the development of talent, and through study and practice."[16] Fromm further defines creativity as "the ability to see (or to be aware) and to respond," regardless of the existence or non-existence of process and product.[17] Moreover, Fromm's ability includes the human capability to be puzzled, to concentrate on or experience one's self, to imagine or fantasy beyond objective reality. And further it includes the ability of coping with objective phenomena such as conflict, anxiety, pain, and so on.

B. A Biblical Perspective on Creativity

According to the Report of the Commission on Theology and Church Relations of the Lutheran Church-Missouri Synod, "creation" refers to creatio ex nihilo (creation out of nothing), good work, and divine pleasure.[18]

(1) Creation out of Nothing. Paul's epistle to the Hebrews reads, "Through faith we understand that the worlds were framed by the word of God, so that things which are seen were not made of things which do appear" (Heb. 11: 3). Creation is to bring forth form from formlessness or light into darkness (Gen. 1: 2; Jer. 4: 23).

41

(2) <u>Goodness of Creation</u>. Moses' first book, Genesis, begins with the good work of God's creation. "God saw it was good" (Gen. 1: 10, 12, 18, 21 and 25). Upon completion of His creation, "God saw every thing that he made, and behold, it was very good" (Gen. 1: 31). Finally, the Psalmist praises God by declaring, "the earth is full of Thy riches" (Ps. 104: 24).

(3) <u>Divine Pleasure of Creation</u>. God blessed and sanctified the sabbath as a holy day (Gen. 2: 3), and commanded man's endeavor not to do any evil (Isa. 56: 2) and to worship and honor God (Isa. 58: 13) on this holy day.

C. Tentative Definition of Creativity

On the basis of psychological and Biblical perspectives on creativity, this writer would like to formulate a definition of "creativity." That is, creativity is human <u>ability</u> to make something new (product), <u>ability</u> to consciously-unconsciously think and imagine (process) potential product in the making, and <u>ability</u> to integrate individual hereditary potentiality and environmental impression into a higher level of life satisfaction-Abraham Maslow's term, "peak-experience." In other words, creativity is the <u>ability</u> which enhances and energizes creative productivity and process; namely, it is the origin of human behavior and the basis of creative product and process.

Creativity further details man's ability to create "something out of nothing," including the ability to create a new synthesis out of existing creatures, although the latter connotes the ability for "discovering" rather than "new making." Art, music, poetry and so on, are originated by man, are consequences of human creativity; and the discoveries of natural law, such as law of gravity, and law of relativity are also consequences of human creativity. The laws of nature are not being made by man, but discovered by man through his cognitive and motivational process. Nevertheless, although man does not create but discovers natural laws, when man makes "something" out of the discovered knowledge, we would indicate that his performance is the exercise of "ability" to make (creativity), since he makes something new (unknown hitherto) out of something known. In this way, human discovery is included in human creativity, and everything which man originally brings to being or existence out of non-being or non-existence, is the consequence of human creativity, and further the testimony of the divine worth of man, wherein lies the power of creation.

Such human ability to make is good, according to the Biblical perspective on creation, and according to H.H. Hart, human creativity is "fundamentally based on love, and on the happy, guilt-free disposal of aggression in socially-acceptable channels."[19] "Good" implies no harm to fellow men and other creatures in the universe, but rather significant benefits for the betterment of fellow men and other creatures. No creativity of man (defined as ability to create) is "bad"; it is good, beautiful and benevolent to fellow men and other creatures. When the ability is misapplied, however, the result is an adverse consequence and distorted expectation. As an example, the human creativity of making a knife is good when it is applied to medicine to extract a malignant tumor inside of the human body; namely, it benefits human health. The same instrument, however, is potential for destructive application when it is placed in the hands of a murderer. The potential consequence of human creativity is contingent upon the utilizer, the applicator, the man, his motivation, intention, and understanding. Accordingly, the consequences of a certain person's creativity, production, theory or ideas, may be either "good" or "better."

Human creativity benefiting human betterment further implies applicability and practicality of creativity in relation to the spatio-temporal finite being of man. In this sense, social utility of human creativity can be classified into good, better or best, rather than good or bad, based on contemporary particular human needs. What is meant here is that from a particular person's point of view, one man's creativity—ability and its product or process such as theory or idea—is more applicable and meaningful than another's; namely, it suggests the relativity, situationality, contingency, of human creativity, rather than "either-or" validity.

"The efforts of individual man are constantly modifying the world of creatures including man himself," reports the aforementioned Commission on Theology.[20] Such human efforts are possible by simple virtue of existence of the human ability to create, which is one of the divine endowments that man received upon being created after the image of God. In Genesis, man was crowned to be the host of the earth (Gen. 1: 28), and divinely ordered to continue God's creation and to preserve all creatures given to man. Man's first creativity, in fact, was revealed in naming the creatures (Gen. 2: 19-20).

Creativity and Human Mind

When we say "mind," the word appears to be ambiguous and easily confused with such words as body, flesh, soul, or heart, especially in the Biblical interpretation of mind. The following Biblical verses call for clarification:

Thou shalt love the Lord thy God with all thy heart, and with all thy soul, and with all thy mind (Matt. 22: 37).

What doeth the Lord thy God require of thee, but to fear the Lord thy God, to walk in all his ways, and to love him, and to serve the Lord thy God with all thy heart, and with all thy soul (Deut. 10: 12).

The Lord thy God will circumcise thine heart, and the heart of thy seed, to love the Lord thy God with all thine heart, and with all thy soul, and thou mayest live (Deut. 30: 6).

Thus mind, soul and heart appear to be all the components of man, or the trinity of man.

Aristotle's conception of soul included the natural development of bodily growth, bodily sensation, and the capacity of thinking, what he called, the vegetative soul, the sensitive soul, and the rational soul, respectively, as though he implied that soul is synonymous with man.[21] He further discussed some characteristics of soul: soul as motion and sensation-sensory-motor activity, which describes every piece of behavior or life itself; soul as the causality of movement; soul as infinite shapes or atoms. Other views include soul as never resting, moving in the air, soul in self-movement; soul as identical with mind (Anaxagoras's view); and soul as constructed out of "idea-number" (Empedocles and Plato) which represents the forms of things-- reason as idea number one (universal), knowledge as two (primary length), opinion as three (breadth), and sensation as four (primary depth).

In the Old testament, soul is interpreted "nephesh" in Hebrew, as life or self, which is "not an entity with a separate nature from the flesh and possessing a capability of a life of its own. Rather it is the life animating the flesh." In this sense, soul is a living being. "Man does not 'have' a soul, he is a soul."[22]

In the New Testament, soul or life ("psyche" in Greek) implies natural immortality and being subject to eternal judgement (Matt. 10: 28 and Luke 12: 4). Therefore, as Mark writes (8: 35-37), the soul is the most precious part of human being because of its magnificent value, in that nothing in the universe has the power to purchase it. Such an immortal and precious soul is the object of God's plan for salvation at the end of human life (Pet. 1: 9)--the potential of being freed from sin, being cleansed, becoming holy and receiving everlasting life (Rom. 6: 22).

It follows, therefore, that soul is the seat for the spirit which belongs to the Creator, the breath of God by which human life is made possible, and the active participant in communication of man with God, conveying mind-body matter to God and vice versa. A Biblical distinction between mind and heart appears to be difficult because in many verses of English translation, both words are employed interchangeably.[23]

The individual human body, however, is the temple of human soul, mind, and heart. It functions in the physical world in accordance with the framework of soul and mind. Namely, it is a physical expression of the existence of human soul and mind. Biblically, the individual body is involved in sin (Rom. 6: 6; 8: 13) and is subject to death (Rom. 8: 10), and accordingly is bound by physical laws (Rom. 7: 5) or by man-made rules and regulations. Furthermore, it is weak and mortal (Ps. 78: 39; Gen. 6: 3; Job 34: 15), for which God bestows His mercy freely and abundantly.

The individual human body involves itself in congregations of men, such as family, group, community, society and nation, where it demonstrates and communicates its unique individuality derived from the functions of soul and mind. In this sense, the body is limited only in unity, not in union--the sphere of soul and mind--which implies actual transformation or absorbence into another body. A body is physiologically independent and unique as it is, and therefore, combination of substances is not necessary, although medically possible. The finitude of human being implies body only, not soul or mind.

A. Review of Theories of Mind

Biblically, the word mind is from the Greek work "syneidsis," meaning "conscience," used in Acts 23: 1, 24: 16, Rom. 2: 15, and in many other verses throughout Paul's epistles to churches and friends. Conscience, in a Biblical interpretation, simply means "good," "sound moral" behavior of man--the source of friendship, love, care, other-mindedness, and so on. Beyond this conscientious nature of mind, Paul indicates the intellectual nature of mind which includes reasoning,

45

thinking, or understanding, and further indicates mind as a tool for the service of God (Rom. 7: 23-25). What is "service of God?" It is continuation of creativity and preservation of all creatures, which is the divine commandment to man. Thus, through the operation of mind, man carries out his divine order. This understanding power of human mind extends its sphere into the spiritual world through ecstatic experience (I Cor. 14: 14)--what Martin Buber calls "meeting ground"--that is, mind is for union, not for unity, of God and man, man and man, man and nature. Such ecstasy, for Paul Tillich, is "the state of mind which is extraordinary in the sense that the mind transcends its ordinary situation...of finite rationality."[24]

Mind is "the cause of universe" which implies that the universe is created by the functioning of mind in regard to natural laws. In the pre-Christian era, two famous philosophers who dealt with theories of soul and mind were Socrates and Lucretius. Socrates writes that the universe at large is "the embodiment, like a properly conducted human life, or coherent rational plan. If mind is the cause of the world's structure, the earth and everything else in the universe must have just the shape, position, place in the scheme, which is 'best' that each of them should have."[25] This mind-ordered universe is called by Socrates "the beautiful," and by Alfred North Whitehead, "the eternal object."[26]

Lucretius, who is known as an existentialist, insisted that the "human power of independent reason to pursue happiness and to overcome the adversities of fate" refers to mind (as synonymous with understanding) as the directing principle over the functions of body and soul, capable of altering the whole man as well as sharing pains together with body and soul:

Mind and the soul are kept together in close union and make up a single native but that the directing principle which we call mind and understanding is the head so to speak and reigns paramount in the whole body. It has a fixed seat in the middle region of the breast; here throb fear and apprehension about these spouts dwell soothing joys; therefore, here is the understanding or mind. All the rest of soul disseminated through the whole body obeys and moves at the will and inclination of the mind.[27]

In the seventeenth century, Thomas Hobber described mind as the motions in certain parts of the organic body, head of which motion proceeds to the heart.[28] About the same time, Rene Descartes wrote the famous words "Cogito, ergo sum,"--"I think, therefore I am"--meaning that thoughts proceeding from the mind are the essence of human existence.

The eighteenth century philosopher David Hume documented "reason" as the major source of the infinite difference between man and other creatures, and described the qualities of mind.[29] The first quality of human mind is sympathy, which implies a perceptive process of mind-conversion of an idea into an impression; namely, a conversion of the faint images of contents in thinking and reasoning into the content of the feeling such as sensation, passions and emotions. The second quality of mind is the power of comparison. The variation of human judgement on an object is contributed by the function of mind which compares the objects in light of the purpose of the function. The third quality of human mind is, according to Hume, independent--in his term, "pride, self-applause." A human mind operates independently without interference from, and without being dependent upon, foreign considerations, such as external stimuli or validation. The operation of human mind is solely associated with conduct, merit, confidence and assurance of life. And further he says, "a genuine and healthy pride or self-esteem, is essential to the character of a man of honor." The last quality of mind is goodness. This is the quality of love, generosity, humanity, compassion, gratitude, friendship, zeal, self-disinterestedness, and liberality.

Based on Descartes and Hume's idea of human mind, William James conceptualized human mind as a theatre of simultaneous and infinite possibilities and thinking, although it was characterized by spatio-temporal variability and mutability. According to James, thought which proceeds from the mind is: (a) "personal," which implies that thoughts are connected with other thoughts but established upon a person's conscious experience; (b) in constant change—"what is got twice is the same object" but "no two ideas are ever exactly the same"; (c) sensibly continuous regardless of a time-gap between "before and after" thought; (d) independent of itself; and (e) a choosing activity and deliberate will-- "no two men ever are known to choose alike."[30]

George Herbert Mead, who was influenced by Dewey, James, Hume, Descartes, Leibnitz, and Aristotle--called the old tradition--developed a notion of human mind as the incorporation of social process.[31] Human mind, for Mead, arises through the internalization of the conversation of significant gestures by the individual in the social processes of experience and behavior. He further contends that human mind not only produces

47

significant symbols, but also is constituted with various possibilities of response to different stimuli. Moreover, such symbols and various responses operate in respect to the future rather than to the past although they are unavoidably associated with the past.

H. H. Horne, in his article "An Idealistic Philosophy of Education," briefly deals with human mind as the ground for accepting idealistic philosophy. For Horne, human mind is the cause of "explanation," which includes raising problems, facing problems, seeking the solutions. Mind as explainer is subjectively used and objectively applied.[32] Horne further expands human mind as being space-free, weight-free, dimension-free directly associated with personal experience, consciousness, and perception of qualities.

Lastly, Martin Heidegger discusses four different qualities of human mind.[33] The first quality of mind is "knower" --in Heidegger's term "mood or Being-attuned," which implies that human mind is disclosed by being-in-the-world as a whole, and directs oneself into something. Secondly, "understanding"--the basic mode of Dasein's Being according to Heidegger. Understanding implies the potentiality which is to become. In this sense, human mind is in the process of becoming and transforming. Thirdly, "interpretation," which implies the power of projection, foresight, conceptualization, of the understanding. And fourthly, "assertion", that is, out of interpretation, human mind makes some judgment including prediction and communication of the inter- pretation.

From a brief look at human mind as described by these numerous philosophers and theoreticians, this writer will draw a conclusion as to what human mind is in respect to creativity. Mind is an incarnated Logos, that is, given to human being--the Logos which existed at the time of creation, and which brought orderliness out of chaos. Human mind which potentially is in pregnancy of human "ability to create" includes intellectuality which implies thinking, imagining, understanding, reasoning, memorizing, decision-making and other mental operations. "Creative man who has not lost the capacity to yearn with his whole being for richer utilities...grows...to glory...rejoices in the truth."[34]

Growth of Human Creativity

Thus, human creativity is a divinely endowed and eternally existing ability in human mind. Then the question is how human

48

creativity grows and develops. What are the necessary conditions for the growth of human creativity?

Upon creation of man, according to Genesis, every single creature was given to man, who was given the highest authority of governance. This transaction between the Creator and man was instituted solely for the purpose of cultivation, preservation, and continuation of creation. The creativity in man is then subject to be bound by divine transactional purposes, and accordingly it has to be cultivated.[35]

With an assumption that some "necessary conditions" for human creativity are sufficiently provided, Charlott Buhler, C.W. Graves, and especially Jean Piaget, discuss a developmental view of human creativity, yet from different aspects--human creativity in terms of "goal setting behavior" (Buhler), "endless transformation" (Grayes), and "assimilation-accommodation process" (Piaget).[36]

According to their developmental view, human creativity begins in the very early life of a human being. Especially, for Buhler, human creativity as goal setting behavior begins in the prenatal period in a form of activity which is "passive yet aggressive." She explains that selective perception, although responsive at times, is observed in infancy--in other words, "innate perceptual pattern" and "innate reference." Then, through various emotional and social experiences, a child (age eight to twelve) becomes able to consolidate his beliefs and values, crystalizes his opinion, and orders principles for himself--(Buhler's "basic tendency"). Upon integrating all life experiences, an individual consciously develops or creates a direction, purpose and meaning, and continues his creative work.

Graves's notion of endless transformation of human existence suggests two major levels of human existence: the level of substance and Being.[37] The level of substance includes human basic needs--physiological, psychological, materialistic, and social--which are not horizontally or vertically distinguished, but rather are "cycling." In the process of cycling, a human being meets his existential needs, and in doing so he thinks, experiences, makes decisions, interprets, and defines, which are some practical revealments of human creativity. Through continuous cycling, man gradually evolves into cognitive existence (first Being), or what Graves calls "Existential Emergence," where the human being is revealed to himself as distinctively different from the animals, and where he exercises his creativity in the form of knowing and doing. At the level of experiential existence (second Being) man develops more confident knowledge and creates himself in rather sophisticated fashion.

Piaget's stage theory reveals the developmental stages of human creativity as well as those in cognition, perception, and morality. His theory could therefore be named "the theory of natural growth." During the first stage (sensori-motor period, 0-2 years), the child senses and acts with little thought, but he develops the ideas of "object permanence." Gradually, toward two years of age, the child begins to use some physical motions in the form of gesture and imitation, and further to behave objectively and independently.

In the second stage (preoperational representation period, 2-7 years), the child develops his ability to use language although his powers of reason may still be insufficient for him to understand relationships such as wife, husband, cousin, and uncle. His behavior is more or less intuitive, without reasoning why he behaves such a way--not able to explain "why" he behaves as he does. The most important development during this period is an internalization of his experience. When he observes an ice cube melting on the stove, he internalizes his observation as an absolute irreversibility; namely, unless he has an experience of observing water transforming into an ice cube, no argument or justification is valid to him--that is, the child has no reasoning ability to reverse his "ice to water" observation.

In the third stage (concrete operation period, 7-11 years), however, the child begins to develop his reasoning power, begins to understand reversibility, and begins to think logically. He further begins to make relationships and to understand the process of transformation (changing process). In the final stage of development (formal operational period, 11-15 years), the child develops the power of inferential thinking, and questions the meaning and potentiality of present observations, from which he may be able to arrive at a new synthesis, i.e., when A B C is observed, the child infers A C through the same observation. This is what Silvano Arieti calls "pars pro toto" which implies inferring, abstracting, constituting, isolating and assimilating the not-given from the given.[38]

One of the issues around suggested theories above, however, is in relation to quantity of human ability to create, since these theories suggest that the growth of human creativity is positively associated with human physiological and chronological development. These theories further suggest that "grown" and "older" individuals are more creative than "less-grown" and "young" individuals, or vice versa, that is, human ability to create develops in accordance with the physiological development of man.

Despite the suggestions of the developmental theories described, there may be an inverse association between human ability and physiological development: some young children are more creative than some adults. However, when we employ such evaluative or judgmental terms as "more-less," "good-bad," and so on, we certainly view creativity as product or possibly process, rather than ability. It is true that creative product or process is a consequence of the exercise of human ability to create and is subject to objectivity or evaluation. But the ability is a human essence beyond objectivity (although it is possible to infer the change, growth or development of ability via observation of creative product or process).

Several inferential frameworks assume a potential developmental pattern of human creativity, or ability to create, which is implied in physiological and chronological human growth. Maslow's study of self-actualizing people, "A Study of Psychological Health" which represent an atypical case study, concludes that human creativity is observed in every sample case without exception, and further that human creativity is a universal characteristic of man.[39] He says that human creativity is a potentiality given to all human beings at birth. Although human acculturation process may have an effect on the developmental course of human creativity, the given human potentiality to create will never die, but live. This given human potentiality at birth or at conception—human creativity—is to grow into a higher level of creativity as an individual human being masters each level of sophistication in the process of sequential maturation. Therefore, the ability to create is given to every human being to cherish and develop, and accordingly its differential measurement between different individual human beings is beyond theoretical description. An evaluative attitude toward human creativity is impossible if creativity is defined as the ability to create. Evaluation of creativity is possible only if it is defined as product or process.

The Characteristics of Human Creativity

Human creativity is characterized by its unique and paramount nature of man's being unable to avoid it, and by its being immortal, continuous, independent, and beyond evaluation.

A.   Unavoidability

Man, being mindful, is finite in some aspects--such as in his spatio-temporal existence. Man is finite also by virtue of his being not able to be un-creative. Upon his conception as potential man, a baby-man grows into the image of God by receiving "mind," the incarnated Logos, the creative power. This is the law of creation and the law of preservation of man, the above-all creature. As Paul Tillich expounds, as long as "creation is not only God's freedom but also His destiny," human creativity is also a divine endowment to be exercised in freedom; and further, it is the destiny of man. Man, thus, is predestined to exercise creativity, through which man preserves purpose of creation and also the divine order to the created man by the Creator. In Tillich's words, "The fulfillment of creation is the actualization of finite freedom," for "man is the 'telos' of creation."[40]

The existential need of man is man's search for "newness." It is not because of uselessness, ugliness or the negative experiences of "oldness," but simply because of the divine essence of man. It is not rejection of oldness, but rather an enhancement of oldness. Man's search for newness is fulfilled in his uniquely owned creativity, the ability to create. Newness is something which is not only made out of nothing, but also an un-covered synthesis of already existing somethings. Creative art, such as aesthetics, music, poetry, and other forms of art, may be characterized as revealment of the former creativity of man, and the discoveries of natural laws and the progress of existing materials, scientific technologies, and human knowledge as the latter creativity of man. This latter creativity of man is described by Tillich with the word "transformation," which is also a God-given power of man, the power of transforming man himself and his world.[41] Tillich, however, adds that man can transform only what is given to him. The aesthetic emotion and the effort of discovering truth are the paramount beauty of man.

B.   Immortality

The most significant human creativity is symbol (Gen. 2: 19). Symbols are different from signs. Signs belong to the usage of image, which exist in the physical world, and are identifiable stimuli (as Gordon Allport defines them) or "reacting toward" (in Susanne Langer's term). [42] In contrast to signs, however, symbols are "self-produced signs of signs" and also "a typical process of thinking"-- not thinking things, but thinking about things. [43] For further distinction between the two, signs are facts and data, while symbols are in the form of imagination, thought, memory, belief beyond experience, dream, hypothesis, philosophy, ideation, metaphor and abstraction.

Langer further suggest two kinds of symbols: <u>presentative</u> and <u>discursive</u>. Presentative symbols are maps, photographs, diagrams, and most of all human language, which is "the most momentous and the most mysterious product of the human mind." Discursive symbols are revealed in such aesthetic expression as art, music, poetry, culture and so on. [44] Whatever the created symbols are, they are immortal, existing side by side along with human existence and human history. All scientific discoveries are continually and potentially pregnant with new knowledge and synthesis, and all human aesthetic significances are bred into other human minds. The works of Michelangelo, the immortal waltzes of Johann Strauss, the beautiful songs of Stephen Foster, the poetry of Henry Longfellow--all simultaneously bear truthful testimony to the immortality of human creation.

The symbols which are the product of human creativity are immortal as long as their maker, man exists in immortality. The immortality of man is described by Margaret Mead in the following three ideas. [45] The first idea is that the period of human life begins from the eternity or at birth (or at conception) and stretches onward to eternity. Examples are the folk beliefs of eastern European Jews, who believe in the pre-existence of soul waiting to be born: that of Palestinian Arabs, believing in the simultaneous creation of earth and soul by angels; that of Christians believing in a repetitive cycle of "dust thou art and unto dust thou shalt return"; and that of Buddhists, believing in reincarnation, or transformation of human life in another sphere, which is revealed in Polynesian and Confucian ancestor worship. The third idea is the Hindu teaching that there is an endless recurrence of personal identity within the same family life. Thus, as man is immortal, so are his creatures.

C. Continuity

According to Martin Heidegger, human creativity involves a time sequence. He describes man as having three constitution-

53

alities in relation to time (Zeit): namely, (a) "ontic," the determinate character of existence, a historical property of man, which is "facticity yet contingency," as C.D. Keyes interprets it; (b) "ontological," man's property in his present existence, in Keyes's term "falling"; and (c) "ontic-ontological," a priority and a possibility for man's future, in Keyes's term "existence, projection." Therefore, Heidegger's ontic constitutionality represents "man," Dasein.[46]

No human creativity is exercised without thinking with a disciplined mind on the basis of facticity (past). Facticity includes history and career and exists always in the process of human creativity. It enhances present creativity into the framework of projection.[47] As a practical example, the human journey to the moon is being materialized at its present level based on the facticities obtained from numerous and pragmatic "experiential" examples of human creativity in the past, and certainly the present level of realization will be brought into the process of human creativity in the future. Therefore, it is called "historic journey" not because of its place in the book of human creativity, but because of its continuing career in disciplined minds. It is called so not because of successful completion of the journey, but because of its valuable facticity potential for infinite human creativity. Human creativity is never made, but is in continuous making. It is more than yesterday, will be even most tomorrow, and should experientially proceed beyond the most.

D. Independence

Being influenced by Jean-Paul Sartre, who said that "the essence of man is his existence," Paul Tillich states, in his book The Courage To Be, that "Man creates what he is. Nothing is given to him to determine his creativity. The essence of his being the 'should-be,' 'the ought-to-be,' is not something which he finds; he makes it. Man is what he makes of himself."[48] Such absolute independence of human creativity is rooted in human mind and revealed in the human symbol-making efforts. Symbol-making process in human mind includes what George Herbert Mead calls "interpretation and definition," which further implies a "formulative process"-- not as a passive response under the influence of the operations of outside stimuli.[49]

Interpretation is not a mere reaction to external stimulus, but a positive action toward it, simply because of the absence of intrinsic and inherited value in the external stimulus.[50]

54

Man does not <u>respond to</u>, but acts <u>toward</u>, in his process of symbol-making. Thus, interpretation is a process of transformation of impressions from external stimuli in a frame of reference of life goals individually set. Nothing can coerce this process without a choice made by the individual person. Therefore, this process makes man wonderful, and it is beyond the control of external manipulation.

Definition is a conclusion arrived at out of interpretation; namely, it is a notion of "let-it-be" and is a mighty order stemming from human power of creation. A house, once defined by man, remains a house maintaining its man-given identity and expectation without resistance. Even a slight change in its identity and expectation will occur only if man gives an appropriate definition for change. Any creature in the universe does not have its inherent value without the touch of human creativity. Thus, by the act of definition, man continues to exercise his creativity, and his creative act is performed without external prescription. Even if his creative act appears to be influenced by an external prescription, he is not truly so influenced. Rather, he chooses to employ an external stimulus to enhance the process of interpretation and definition. This is an essential prerogative of man, and originates from human ability to create.

E.   Evaluation

The incarnation of Logos is revealed in the form of human logic and reason--powers with which man comes to think, decide, develop, make, describe, interpret, define, uncover, discover, challenge, question, and so on, all of which are manifestations of human creativity. When such creativity is symbolized for empirical observation, the products or processes of human creativity are subject to measurement, evaluation and valuation. People are quick to criticize another's creative productivity by categorizing it into a continuum of good or bad, poor or rich, and so on. Every creative product, however, is noble in this universe, regardless of its maker, either young or old, male or female, black or white, "retarded" or "brilliant." It is valuable in the universe due to its nature of being infinitely different from any other creative product.

An emotionally disturbed child wrote a poem: <u>The Day is Bea-u-ti-ful</u>:

It is blue up there
And blue down here

55

I am up there
And I am down here
Where it is blue,
The day is bea-u-ti-ful.

The sky is blue and not black
The wind is soft and not hard
The clouds are white and not black
Such a bea-u-ti-ful day
No more doggone ugly songs
Going round and round in my head.[51]

Is this poetry to be evaluated or measured? Or should it be? No, simply because it is the product of an invaluable human being, and does not seek any validation of its inherent value. When creative product is beyond valuation, the human ability to create which brings creative product into the objective reality is further beyond valuation. Appreciation is an impetus for stirring and constructing human creativity. A poem by an emotionally disturbed child; five-year old Mozart's incomparable piano piece; the adult Beethoven's penetrating fifth and ninth symphonies written despite his physiological impairment; Tchaikovski's rich "Poetic Symphony"; Johann Strauss's waltz music; the great drama of Shakesphere; the immortal music of Stephen Foster, capturing the spirit of America; the decaying hut in Africa and the high-rise building in New York--each and all have unique value and sanctity that evoke appreciation, not valuation. Regardless of age, health, locality, economic and social status, productions of human creativity are beyond human valuation but deserve the richest human appreciation. For Sartre, "beauty is a value applicable only to the imagination and which means the negation of the world in its essential structure."[52]

SUMMARY

Men, as Maslow has said, "are relatively unfrightened by the unknown, the mysterious, the puzzling, and often are positively attracted by it, i.e., selectively pick it out to puzzle over, to meditate on, and to be absorbed to." He continues, "Men do not neglect the unknown, or deny it, or run away from it, or try to make believe it is really known, nor do they cling to the familiar, nor is their quest for the truth a catastrophic need for certainty, safety, definiteness, and order."[53]

The divine endowment of human creativity implies human ability to "make" (creatio ex nihilo) and human ability to experience "goodness and pleasure." This God-given human creativity originates from human mind, the incarnated Logos, whose functions are ordering exercise--intellectual exercise, moral exercise and communion. Human creativity is eternal, its existence is from eternity to eternity. Some scholars such as Buhler, Graves, Piaget, Arieti and Maslow theorize that human creativity is revealed in every man at the earliest stage of life (either conception or birth), and grows into higher and higher sophistication of creativity. Creativity is universal to every human being, making man human, not an animal.

Some characteristics of human creativity are as follows: First, human creativity is the unavoidable exercise of human being. It is a consequence of divine transaction upon created men, compelling him to be creative. Secondly, human creativity is immortal. It remains in the hearts of man and establishes heart-to-heart communication in the form of art, music, literature, culture, religion and so on. Thirdly, human creativity has a career of transformal development. It is not a sudden accomplishment, but a consequence of synthesis of the available creativities in a temporal sequence shared with the Logos of eternity. Fourthly, human creativity is independent, for it is rooted in the operation of human mind. Man alone exercises his ability to create in light of his creative goal. This goal is revealed as process or product. Therefore, to be creative, man does not require external manipulation, but rather requires the availability of external stimuli to be utilized according to man's free choice. And lastly, human creativity is beyond valuation. No human creativity is bad, but made to be good in the Biblical sense, regardless of the human racial, chronological, biological, physiological, social and economic characteristics of individual man.

In the Biblical sense, human creativity originated at the time of creation. It is subjectively validated by human mind as it exists in human reality. Man possesses his creative ability from heredity and receives impressions from experience. His ability and imported impressions together become his uniquely and personally owned "brick," the subjective framework of his creativity. With this "transformed-yet-transforming" brick, man materializes his mindful exercise of creativity in reality. Consequently, the consistent creativity of man is sovereign within personality. In essence, a creative self asserts that man makes his own personality--which is subjectively, unifiedly, and uniquely stylized. Such personality gives meaning of life, and creates the individual goal of life as well as the means to the goal—the active principle of individual human life. Man is rightfully and dutifully to exercise his ability to create. This makes man human, the host of the universe.

FOOTNOTES

1. See Calvin W. Taylor, _Creativity: Progress and Potential_ (New York, 1964), p. 2.

2. J. P. Guilford, "Factors that Aid and Hinder Creativity," in E. Paul Torrance, et al., _Creativity: Its Educational Implication_ (New York, 1967), p. 107.

3. Rollo May, "Nature of Creativity," in _Creativity and Its Cultivation_, ed. Harold H. Anderson (New York, 1959), p. 59. See also Taylor, _Creativity_, p. 2, and Torrance, et al., _Creativity_, p. 1.

4. Taylor, _Creativity_, p. 7.

5. As quoted from E. Paul Torrance, et al., _Creativity_, p. 2.

6. Richard S. Crutchfield, "The Creative Process," in _Proceedings of the Institute of Personality Assessment and Research_, University of California (Berkeley, 1961), p. VI-I.

7. J. P. Guilford, "Three Faces of Intellect," in _Readings in Classroom Learning_, ed. Sherman H. Grey and Earl S. Haugen (New York, 1969), pp. 186-205.

8. See Calvin W. Taylor, _Widening Horizons in Creativity_, (New York, 1964), pp. 112-113.

9. William J. J. Gordon, _Synectics_ (New York, 1961), pp. 33-35.

10. The quotation is from Rollo May, "Nature of Creativity," p. 59.

11. Carl R. Rogers, "Toward a Theory of Creativity," in _Creativity_, ed. Anderson, p. 71.

12. Harold H. Anderson, "Creativity as Personality Development," in _Creativity_, ed. Anderson, pp. 119-121.

13. The term "novelty" is used by Carl Rogers. See Rogers, "Toward a Theory of Creativity," p. 73.

14. Morris I. Stein and Shirley J. Hainze, _Creativity and the_

Individual (Chicago, 1960), pp. 203, 215-216.

15. Ibid., p. 236.

16. Leonard Steinberg, "Creativity as a Character Trait: An Expanding Concept," in Creativity: Its Educational Implications, ed. Torrance, et al., p. 124.

17. The quotation is from Eric Fromm, "The Creative Attitude," in

Creativity, ed. Anderson, p. 44.

18. The Lutheran Church-Missouri Synod, Commission on Theology and

Church Relations, Creation in Biblical Perspective: A Report,
p. 4.

19. Stein and Heinze, Creativity and the Individual, pp. 193-194.

20. The quotation is from the Lutheran Church-Missouri Synod, Creation in Biblical Perspective, p. 12.

21. Floyd W. Matson, Being, Becoming and Behavior (New York, 1967), p. 23.

22. J. Hastings, ed. Dictionary of the Bible (New York, 1963). "soul", p. 392.

23. See for example, Job 27:6, Exod. 4:21, Deut. 2:30, Josh. 11:20, Ezk. 18:31, Deut. 9:6, 1 King 11:4, Matt. 5:8, 2 Tim.
2:22, 1 Pet. 1:22, 1 Tim. 4:2, Luke 8: 15, 1 John 3:20.

24. Paul Tillich, Systematic Theology I (Chicago 1965), pp. 111-112.

25. Taylor, Socrates, p. 54.

26. Ibid., p. 148.

27. Matson, Being, Becoming and Behavior, pp. 31-33.

28. Ibid., p. 37.

29. David Hume, Treatise of Human Nature (Oxford, 1739), pp.

592-605.

30. William James, The Principles of Psychology, vol. I (New York, 1890), pp. 225-290.

31. George Herbert Mead, Mind, self and Society, ed. C.W. Morris
(Chicago, 1934), "introduction" and pp. 118-192.

32. H.H. Horne, "An Idealistic Philosophy of Education,"
Philosophy of Education, 41st Year Book, part I (Washington,
National Society for the Study of Education), pp. 172-199.

33. Martin Heidegger, Being and Time, trans. J. MacQuarrie and E.
Robinson (New York, 1962), pp. 172-199.

34. H.L. Parson, "Rooted and Grounded in Love," in The Nature of
Man, ed. Simon Doniger (New York, 1962), p. 84.

35. "Be cultivated" implies being provided with the necessary conditions for creativity which eventually contributes to the
approximation of creative potentials.

36. See, for the necessary conditions for creativity, James F.T. Bugental, "Precognition of a Fossel," Journal of Humanistic Psychology 2 (Fall 1962): 41-42. See also Charlott Buhler, "Human Life Goals in the Humanistic Perspective," Journal of Humanistic Psychology 7 (Spring 1967): 36-52; C.W. Graves, "Levels of Existence: An Open System Theory of Values," Journal of Humanistic Psychology 10 (Fall 1970): 131-155; Jean Piaget, The Moral Judgment of the Child (Glencoe, Ill., 1948); and Langdon E. Longstreth, Psychological Development of the Child (New York, 1968), pp. 154-159.

37. Graves, "Levels of Existence," 133.

38. The term "pars pro toto" is used by Silvano Arieti, "Toward a Unifying Theory of Cognition, "General Systems 10 (1965); 112.

39. Abraham Maslow, Motivation and Personality (New York, 1970), pp. 149-180.

40. Paul Tillich, Systematic Theology I (Chicago, 1965), p. 256.

41. Ibid., pp. 155-156.

42. See Gordon W. Allport, "Scientific Models and Human Morals," Psychological Review 54(July 1947): 189, and Susanne K. Langer, Philosophy in a New Key (Cambridge, Mass., 1967), p. 57.

43. Allport, "Scientific Models," 189.

44. Langer, Philosophy in a New Key, p. 56.

45. Margaret Mead, "The Immortality of Man," in The Nature of Man, ed. Simon Doniger.

46. See C. D. Deyes, "Truth of Art: An Interpretation of Heidegger's Sein and Zeit and Der Urstrung Des Kunstwekes," in Heidegger and the Path of Thinking, ed. John Sallis (Duquesne University Press, 1970), pp. 65-80.

47. Jean-Paul Sartre, Of Human Freedom, ed. Wade Baskin (New York, 1966), pp. 56-68.

48. Paul Tillich, Courage To Be (New Haven, 1953), p. 148.

49. Herbert Blumer, Symbolic Interactionism: Perspective and Method (Englewood Cliffs, 1969).

50. Ibid.

51. Clark Moustakas, "Honesty, Idiocy, and Manipulation," Journal of Humanistic Psychology 2 (Fall 1962): 32.

52. Sartre, Of Human Freedom, p. 30.

53. Abraham Maslow, Toward a Psychology of Being (New York, 1968), p. 138.

Chapter IV

THE FREEDOM OF MAN

Each person is what he chooses
As being his desire and joy:
Each person is what he strives for
As his enjoyment.
There must be something significant
To what one chooses as his portion:
And shall it prove, then,
To be only vanity?
So what shall now be my choice?
What shall my portion signify?
Thee, Jesus, my crown,
Thee will I prize eternally.

Of two things, choose one;
Indeed, more you cannot have:
And if you choose nothing,
The world does bury you,
And it eventually passes away
With all its lusts,
And what here pleased you
Will fill your breast with sorrow.

Kierkegaardian Hymn,
The Single Choice

Determinism and Freedom

One of the major and endless arguments among philosophers
and between two major traditional schools of psychology, the
Lockean and the Leibnitzian, is in the area of human freedom,
"determinism and freedom," or "negation of human freedom and
sanction of human freedom."

A.   Negation of Human Freedom

Albury Castell in his book The Self in Philosophy presents
several brief passages from the books and articles written by
religious leaders, philosophers and behavioral psychologists,

63

such as Martin Luther, Friedrich Nietzsche, Hans Vaihinger, Ivan Pavlov, Sigmund Freud, and Leslie White.[1] All appear to negate human freedom on the basis of God's immutable, eternal and infallible will (Luther), on the basis of delusion (Nietzsche), of fiction (Vaihinger), of illusion (Freud), of stimulus-conditioned reflexion (Pavlov) and on the basis of cultural independence (White).

These authors and their profound concepts have influenced their followers, such as behavioral psychologists D.O. Hebb, K.S. Lashley, J.B. Watson, A.P. Weiss, Donald Williams, and B.F. Skinner. All alike endeavor to mechanize man structurally and systematically physiologize man into electron-proton formation, which consequently treats man as a material thing, an animal and a plant. Especially Skinner, who is known as a leading behaviorist today, has composed a symphony of utopian world government, "Walden Two," by orchestrating all behavioral concepts together, and proposes a human behavioral technology, "reinforcement within the control," applicable to the construction of a workable, effective and productive pattern of government under which man can exercise his power of choice without catastrophic failure.[2] In another well known book Science and Human Behavior, Skinner powerfully advocates the survival and path of science—science "to paint more realistic pictures."[3] For Skinner, the existence of science is contingent upon the multiplicity and variety of assumptions or hypotheses ("if's") demanded for the sake of science. He pleads that to study man scientifically man's behavior should be manipulated in such a way that scientific technology may be able to handle it, and in doing so, the assumption that "human behavior is lawful and determined" is a mandatory condition. Consequently the exercise of human freedom, will of choice, should be repudiated in science, and yet man does not have even his freedom to be repudiated. As Skinner states it, "the hypothesis that man is not free is essential to the application of scientific method to the study of human behavior." Skinner further asserts that man and animal are exactly identical in all aspects except one, which is the greater complexities of verbal behavior of man. He adds, therefore, that a discussion on the subject of human freedom is not only absurd, but unnecessary interference with scientific analysis of human behavior.[4]

In his most recent book, Beyond Freedom and Dignity, Skinner discusses freedom in terms of "escape" or "counter-attack" of an organism.[5] He presents man as a species whose genetic endowment is breathing, sweating, or digesting food, and who is unavoidably "contingent-upon" external push or stimulus.[6] He presents the human mode of escape from external threat or trouble in the behavior of a slave whipped, of a child nagged by parents, of a victim threatened by a blackmailer, and in the behavior of a student being punished by the teacher.[7] Another mode of escape, for Skinner, is counterattack to reduce or destroy the power of the controllers, manifested in the behavior of a child standing up to his parents, a citizen overthrowing a government, a communicant reforming a religion, a student attacking a teacher or vandalizing a school, and a dropout working to destroy a culture. Thus, he sees human freedom either as a withdrawal or aggression.

Skinner further argues, on the basis of productive labor and work incentives, that human freedom never exists, in that, the slave works to avoid the consequences of not working, the student studies to escape the consequences of not studying, and the worker on "piece work pay"[8] is induced merely to work more per unit of pay. Where is human freedom? Skinner would answer, "Nowhere." Man is not free at all, even has no freedom to be repudiated, says Skinner.

Skinner supplements his point of view with a quote from Emile by Jean-Jacques Rousseau, which reads:

Let (the child) believe that he is always in control, though it is always you (the teacher) who really controls. There is no subjugation so perfect as that which keeps the appearance of freedom, for in that way one captures volition itself. The poor baby, knowing nothing, able to do nothing, having learned nothing, is he not at your mercy? Can you not arrange everything in the world which surrounds him? Can you not influence him as you wish? His work, his play, his pleasures, his pains, are not all these in your hands and without his knowing? Doubtless he ought to do only what he wants, but he ought to want to do only what you want him to do; he ought not to take a step which you have not foreseen; he ought not[9] to open his mouth without your knowing what he will say.

Skinner asserts that his scientific technology of control, reinforcement, is essential to the welfare of the species. Nevertheless, he asserts that "control is clearly the opposite of freedom, and if freedom is good, control must be bad." He therefore continues, "The problem is to free men, not from control, but from certain kinds of control." Then, since the control of external stimuli is so mighty that human freedom is questioned, Skinner concludes, "We do not need to destroy the environment or escape from it; we need to redesign it"--back to the thesis of <u>Walden Two</u>, the world of happy control.[10]

B.   Sanction of Human Freedom

In contrast to the schools of thought negating human freedom, there are equally as many philosophers and psychologists who profess their sanction of human freedom, such as Soren Kierkegaard, Jean-Paul Sartre, Paul Tillich, and Herbert Bonner, and social workers such as Jessie Taft, Virginia Robinson, Helen Perlman, and Eileen Younghusband.

Kierkegaard, who is not only known as the father of existential philosophy but also as the "Apostle of Freedom," employs "leaps" as his earlier terminology implying human freedom including the matters of resolution, decision, determinaiton, conviction, venture, and commitment.[11] For Kierkegaard, human freedom is a divine endowment granted to man; moreover, it is most tremendous because it is "the only language in which God wills to have intercourse with man."[12] For man, no choice is not to choose, which further implies that man can not only choose but is confronted with multiplicity and variability of choice in his life.

Kierkegaard's hallmark, anti-intellectualism, is to proclaim human reason as dependent upon the strength and stability of human conviction, an exercise of human freedom. For Kierkegaard, human reasoning has no right, no power, no authority and no competence to choose and to even know oneself before God, and further it cannot provide any answer to infinite, complicated and urgent human problems. He says:

If I truly have a conviction (and that, we know, is an inner determination in the direction of spirit), my conviction to me is always stronger than reasons: actually, conviction is what supports the reasons, not the other way around . . . he makes a choice; under the weight of responsibility before God, a conviction will be born in him by God's help . . . Reason does not motivate conviction; conviction motivates the reasons.[13]

Similarly, Jesus' conviction and compassion for the sick far transcended human rationalization based on Old Testament Laws.[14] Human reason or knowledge of law, in other words, was weaker than the conviction, thought in freedom, that man is

66

destined to have. Therefore, Kierkegaard re-worded Socrates' "Know Thyself" into "Choose Thyself."

Kierkegaard's life motto was "den Enkelte"--Single One, solitary individual, "to will one thing" -- which implies man to be "an individuality before God." Further, Kierkegaard's indivi- duality not only went beyond the capacity to think (as Descartes says, Cogito, ergo sum), but was also the center of choice, responsibility, repentance and sensitivity. This individuality was consequently known to "the all-knowing One", God, and is transformed into Single One ("God-Individual") whereupon accordingly an individual becomes "the all-knowing one." Such "den Enkelte" was established only through and in the mercy of God who initiates the relationship, not man-to-God, but God-to-Man (John 3:16, 17:16-18). Thus, "no third person dares venture to intrude upon this accounting between God and the individual."[15]

"Den Enkelte" is worldly revealed in the form of simple life, neighborly love, and "Gemeinde" (community). Simple life is of nonconformity to the world, trusting and seeking God's kingdom and His righteousness as described in the Sermon on the Mount (Matt. 5, 6, and 7). Such life is that of poverty, sacrifice, destitution, truly the ascetic life (no thought for worldly life), free from material anxiety (Matt. 6:25-34). Neighborly love, for Kierkegaard, was the duty of man in loving his fellow men. This love is limitless and unchanging regardless of a change in the part of the other persons, also men. And further, this loving is the commandment of God, "Owe no man anything, but to love one another," (Rom. 13:8).

Lastly, "den Enkelte" is revealed in "Gemeinde," or community, where individual conflict gives way to high morality. "Den Enkelte" is not necessarily organizational religion, but man's redemptive relationship to God in Jesus Christ.

Kierkegaard's "den Enkelte," which eternally and naturally contains the nature of humah freedom, influenced Martin Buber. Buber proclaimed human dialogue, and incorporated human sociality as an integral aspect of den Enkelte, which is re-named in his terms "Regina." He interpreted "den Enkelte" as follows:

The single one is not the man who has to do with God essentially, and only unessentially with others, who is unconditionally concerned with God and conditionally with the body politic. The Single One is the man for whom the

67

reality of relation with God as an exclusive relation includes and encompasses the possibility of relation with all otherness, and for whom the whole body politic, the reservoir of otherness, offers just enough otherness for him to pass his life with it.[16]

Thus, for Buber, Regina is always the dialogue between I-and-Thou, man-to-man, and man-to-nature relationship, through which man eventually reaches to God. In short, for Buber, "God wants us to come to him by means of the Reginas He has created and not by renunciation of them."[17]

Jean-Paul Sartre rather powerfully describes human freedom as "the given" by saying that man is "condemned to be free" which implies that no limits to human freedom can be found except freedom itself, and that man is not free to cease being free. "Man cannot be sometimes slave and sometimes free; he is wholly and forever free or he is not free at all..."[18] This further implies man's finite quality, not capable of accepting "not-to-choose." Even an individual who does not choose chooses "not-to-choose," that is, he makes up his mind not to choose. As Kierkegaard claims, for Sartre also, human life is the manifestation of the choosing exercise of man even though man chooses a wrong alternative at times.

By virtue of the infinite potential in man, man has to be free to approximate his potentiality. Human freedom itself, thus, is the vehicle to accomplish maximum materialization of human potentiality, the vehicle that energizes itself without any input or stimulus. For Sartre, this is freedom: "the nothingness which is made-to-be at the heart of man and which forces human reality to make itself instead of to be."[19] Freedom is not a being but a being of man; therefore, it is an unanalyzable totality which triggers the movement of human potentiality. Freedom itself represents the causes, movements, and ends. And therefore, the mode of apprehending causes, motions and ends should originate from the same spirit of freedom. A particular creativity is in the making with assistance not from de-totalized fragments of manipulation but from conscious operation of human freedom. Thus, human action itself is testimony of the existence of human freedom, and human freedom is human action.

Sartre further expounds the giveness of human freedom in relation to the situation of human reality which he calls "facticity of freedom." He says, "There is freedom only in a situation, and there is a situation only through freedom." Such facticity of freedom as the given is revealed in such ways as "place, past, environment, fellow men, and death." Place is a living spot, and past is a prior phenomenon, yet not a determinant of consequent phenomenon, but an illumination of the present in terms of future projection, and accordingly the essence that is "was gewessen ist," what has been. Environment is made up instrumental things which have meaning only in and through the free choice. Fellowship enables individual man to grow with significant meaning, and death (pure fact as is worth) is the final boundary of human life. These facticities, however, become the givens as consequence of the exercise of human freedom, although human freedom is not totally unbounded. It is finite in facticity, yet unlimited within the finitude.[20]

In relation to "finitude and unlimitedness" of human freedom, Sartre and Tillich agree on human freedom as the basic structure of man and its finitude, but disagree regarding the "unlimited" nature of human freedom; namely, for Sartre it is unlimited; for Tillich, limited. Further, for Tillich, human freedom is the unchangeable element in man which makes man not be changed, but it is simultaneously finite and limited by virtue of man's finitude.[21] His notion of "unchangeability" in man is synonymous to his notion of "essence" of man rather than "existence" of man. Essence implies the true and undistorted quality beyond interference of valuation but being reached by abstraction or intuition, whereas existence implies "whatever exists," that is, "stands out" of mere potentiality, is more than it is in the state of mere potentiality and less than it could be in the power of its essential nature.[22] Thus, the exercise of human freedom, the unchangeable essence in man, makes man of humanity, not of zoological animality. Although human estrangement is a negative consequence of such exercise, man is the one who can transcend estrangement, who chooses to be being estranged, and who enhances estrangement for the enrichment of life.

Tillich sees human freedom as the center of the self. The self in the world has a power of self-transformation as well as a power of creation which is capable of transcending every given situation by asking qualities and receiving demands, by making tools, by creating languages, and consequently by creating culture and civilization. For Tillich, the self is the arena of manifestation of human deliberation, decision making, and reception and treatment of stimulus. The self, therefore, accordingly is free to contradict his own nature, to fall away from what he essentially is and ought to be, to try to escape from himself and his true being into sickness in body and mind, into narrowness of compulsive self-seclusion, into imaginary worlds, into what everybody does and everybody thinks, into self- estrangement and hostility. But the center of the self (human freedom) is unchangeable.[23]

Freud's concept of sublimation is interpreted by Tillich as a manifestation of human freedom, a "qualitatively new and a creative act, and this means freedom." Tillich says, "Sublimation is the act which transforms something not sublime into something sublime." He explains that "sublime is a concept which deserves highest standing in formulating a philosophy of life"--the greatest potentiality of life. In the process of sublimation, man continually exercises "decision-making," and his freedom is the source of it.[24]

"Man is a decision-making being who in choosing is faced by the terrifying possibility that the outcome of his choice is highly problematic," says Herbert Bonner. And further Bonner suggests three major evidences of the existence of human freedom: direct experience, biological organization, and moral behavior.[25]

Direct experience implies a man's engagement in acts according to his conscious intention and personal meaning of act and performance, not by "internal or external push" but by "reflection, determination, evaluation and selection of stimulus." Such experience of man, for Bonner, is the fundamental cause of guilt, regret, shame, responsibility and anxiety, and further is a measure of choosing exercise. The biological organization of man, as with all organic life, is protoplasm, which implies a system of self-regulation and goal seeking. For Bonner, the self-regulating and goal-seeking system is not a superstitious or vitalistic explanation but a scientifically defensible hypothesis. He explains human protoplasm as beyond comparison with other ones because of its deliberate and conscious nature. Although man cannot successfully accomplish what he chooses, he is distinctively free to make the deliberate effort regardless of the potential tragedy he may have to experience. All animals instinctly respond to right or wrong food, but only man consciously enriches right food, or modifies wrong food in accordance with his choice to make it as supplemental food. Man faces, acts toward, and challenges specific predicaments, and enhances them for the individuality and uniquely designed existential human life. According to Bonner, another distinction of human

70

protoplasm from other living creatures is that man lives in a remote distant goal. His choice is always for the future, and therefore it carries "the character of novelty, of the unforeseen, of the creative act pointing toward the future." The last evidence of human freedom, according to Bonner, is moral behavior of man, which is the highest (if not supreme) manifestation of volition, deliberation and choice. Bonner claims that "unless man is free to choose his conduct, moral behavior is impossible," although moral behavior is in many cases socially and culturally imposed. Man is not driven to be moral, but he chooses to be moral because moral behavior is humanly desirable instrisically.[26]

C. Critical Comment

(1) "I can do all things through Christ who strengthened me," (Phil. 4:13).

As previously stated, Castell presents Martin Luther's passage from Luther's book The Bondage of the Will, which impresses readers as though there is no human freedom at all.[27] Luther's free will, however, is distinctively different from Nietzsche's free will as calculable and mechanical supposition. It is also different from Vaihinger's as-if fiction, Freud's scientific validation, Pavlov's manipulability and White's puppet of culture. None of these even resembles Luther's free will, which is the absolute, sublime, eternal and original existence in Logos. Logos is beyond calculation, beyond non-being (un-real), beyond science, beyond control and beyond culture. Rather, it is One by Self. It is eternally transformed into man, and man's logos exists in the Logos as the unlimited freedom in the finitude (Sartre) or the limited freedom in the finitude (Tillich). The apostle Paul's assertion that "I can do all things" implies "no limit"; and "through" implies a condition--the "limitation and finitude" of the man. Thus, Luther does not negate freedom of man but rather accepts the limitation and finitude of man within God's absolute free-will. In short, Luther's free will is not the absolute freedom of man but of God, and the others are man's predicaments. The incarnated free will, in the faith of Luther, led to his protest against Catholicism and, ultimately, to the Reformation.

The doctrine of predestination or foreordination propounded by Luther and Calvin is often misinterpreted or misquoted with an implication of "no freedom" of man. Predestination or foreordination, which is known as "Divine Teleology," is from the Greek word "prooriz" meaning "defining, determining beforehand," (Rom. 8:27 and 30; Eph. 1:5; Acts 4:28; and 1 Cor. 2:7). The word itself is related to such words as foreknown, determined, ordained, appointed, purposed, chosen, elected, and so on.

Divine teleology--a theological position--is truly Biblical, rooted in the sole purpose and plan of God for man, God's will toward man. Man is predestined by God's will, but God's will is centered in seeking and saving lost souls. The Bible is nothing but the plan of salvation of man in which God's will is manifested. "Thy will be done on earth as it is in heaven," (Matt. 6:10) implies that men are predestined to be children of God (Rom. 8:21; John 8:32-36; Gal. 5:1) by being set free from the bondage of idols (1 Cor. 12:2; Habak. 2:18), by being ransomed (Mark 10:45; 1 Tim. 2:6) and by being liberated (Isa. 61:1; Luke 4:18). Thus, "Where the Spirit of the Lord is, there is freedom" (2 Cor. 3:17). Consequently, a child of God, man in the image of God, is free, and shall remain in freedom, that is, man is predestined to be free. Thus, predestination is for the salvation of man, salvation from the wrong exercise of human freedom (Gen 2:15-17). When man disobeys, he shall die; when he obeys, he shall live. "Shall" is "predestined"; no man can do anything about it, except say, "I can do all things through Christ who strengtheneth me."

(2) Man is originally created differently from other creatures. One of many differences is that man is created in such a way that he not only sees but looks at, not only hears but listens to, and not only touches but feels. Besides, by virtue of the operation of human mind, the inputs through "look at," "listen to" and "feel" are transformed into unique outputs in various forms of impression, interpretation, comprehension, definition, choice, and so on, in accordance with the different frameworks of individual men. Thus, one of many human predicaments is "to hear without understanding, see without any perceiving," (Isa. 6:9).

From Rousseau's book Emile, Skinner derives the idea of "the power of positive reinforcement" and the benevolence of teachers' exercise of absolute control. Many (including the writer) would agree with Skinner's interpretation of the passage, but at the same time, we might be blind to Rousseau's intention. The authentic meaning of the passage would be "Rousseau's Charge" to teachers to cultivate the soil of the minds of their young and fresh seeds (students); namely, in what he is saying, the magnitude of the teacher's responsibility is subtly stated, rather than deceptive control by "sheep-skinned-goat" identity of teachers. To teach is not to confiscate freedom, but to enhance freedom in the learning process.

Thus, first, Luther's Free-Will implies the Free-Will of God which is for human salvation. Luther's concept of predestination is related to salvation for the lost, life or death in accordance to human obedience or disobedience to God's Free-Will.

Secondly, Skinner's insight from Emile could not be the totality of what Rousseau endeavors to communicate to his readers; namely, Rousseau pleads for teachers' committed attitude to the young and innocent minds of pupils, rather than teachers' deceptive control over pupil's learning.

The Nature of Human Freedom

What is human freedom, then, which is necessarily subject to negation or sanction by so many scientists and philosophers attempting to maintain their creativity in the production of masterpieces? What would be the various manifestations of human freedom?

A. Divine Predestination

Biblically, man is made to exercise his freedom, or incarnated Logos, and for Sartre therefore "to choose" is the divine predicament of man. Allusions to human freedom are read throughout the entire Bible in a series of decision-making, or choosing. Adam and Eve chose to eat the fruit of the tree; Cain chose to kill his brother Abel (Gen. 4); Abraham decided to take what Lot did not choose; people chose not to hear Elijah (1 Kings 18); Ruth decided to move to Bethlehem with her mother-in-law, Naomi (Ruth 1); Jesus' disciples chose to follow Him by giving up their ordinary vocations; Judas chose to betray Jesus; and many more examples might be cited. Thus, Biblically, the history of man is a history of choice, or exercise of God-given freedom. In this way, man is predestined to choose. He is not free not to exist or not to be free.[28]

Another Biblical implication of human freedom is that it is genuine, noble and unhindered. It implies being free from death (Ps. 88:5), a noble use of human freedom for a noble cause (2 Thess. 3:1), "as free, and not using your liberty for a cloak of

73

maliciousness, but as the servants of God" (1 Pet. 2:16), so as not to be "entangled with the yoke of bondage" (Gal. 5:1).

Thus human freedom is a way of human life, and also is the foundation of man's dignity, creativity, morality and future. In free spirit, man is dignified, man thinks and reasons, man acts responsibly, and man designs his future. Without this freedom, man is not human, but an animal. The history of mankind tells us stories of bloody battles for the sake of freedom. Human freedom is not to escape from, or counterattack, bondage, but the choice of whether to escape or to counterattack. External and internal limitations of human freedom are illegitimate but inescapable, yet human freedom consciously faces them and utilizes them toward human construction rather than falling back on them in human destruction. In this way, man remains to be man and preserves his identity of human being. "Everything can be taken from a man but one thing--the last of the human freedoms--to choose one's attitude in any given set of circumstances, to choose one's own way."[29]

> When now a child of man
>   In this short life
> Considers now and then
>   To whom he shall give himself
> God or his enemy,
>   So is the number of days
> For this great choice
>   Appointed by his Friend...
> God Himself makes him brave
>   So that he conquers,
> Reveals to him the noble crown
>   And metes out for him the time,
> That in this conflict he
>   May bring off the prize.

-Alexander Mack, Jr.-

B. Will to Choose

Many books and articles are written by persons who advocate the independence of cultural and environmental factors in relation to human behavior, by proclaiming biological predetermination of man as well as by asserting man as having been acculturated. By virtue of unavoidability of the influence of culture and environment, no one can nullify their provocative proclamation and assertion. These same persons, however, appear

74

to be staggering at the point where they once willed to reach, and never endeavor to step forward beyond the point of stagnation with a simple reasoning about the "will" of man, rather than burying it under the questionable assumption that it does not exist.

Some writers are never contented with such philosophical stagnation. One is Otto Rank, for example. Rank's "will therapy" is rooted in a philosophical premise of human will. Rank believes human will is the maker of human reality, and therefore, "will" is true reality of man. Furthermore, by virtue of existence of human will, man is making his own fate consciously. There is "no fate in an external sense, but to accept and affirm oneself as fate and fate creating power."[30] Such concepts as human will and fate, joined with the functional school of social work in the 1900's as presented by Jessie Taft and Virginia Robinson, contributed to the development of social work concepts such as self-determination, use of will, relationship dynamics and so on.[31]

C. Intention

The word itself is synonymous with "intent, purpose, design, aim, end, object, objective, volition, goal." According to Webster:

Intention implies little more than what one has in mind to do or bring about; intent suggest clearer formulation or more deliberation; purpose suggests more settled determination; design implies a more carefully calculated plan; aim adds to these implications of effort directed toward attaining or accomplishing; end stresses the intended effect of action often in distinction or contrast to the action or means as such; object may equal end but more often applies to a more individually determined wish or need and may nearly approach motive; objective implies something tangible and immediately attainable; goal suggest something attained only by prolonged effort and hardship.[32]

Intentionality as a manifestation of human freedom thus implies human tendency rooted in a process of scrutiny within the human mind—purposive determination and end-goal oriented planning in the presence of consciousness: Namely, it is directional, and meaningful to an individual man, and therefore as Tillich has explained it, intentionality is "being directed toward meaningful content." For Tillich, "only man has complete vitality because he alone has complete intentionality....Man lives 'in' meanings, in that which is valid logically, aesthetically, ethically, religiously."

Intentionality as "directional-to-meaning" is described in Viktor Frankl's experiental novel, Man's Search for Meaning. A Judeo-Christian existentialist, Frankl lived in a spirit of what is called "existential dilemma," meaning "live to suffer, survive to seek meaning." His intentionality transcended beyond the well guarded iron fence of the Auschwitz concentration camp by seeking the meaning of his survival. It may sound absurd, but he says, "An abnormal reaction to abnormal situation is normal behavior." From his "as-if-absurd" experience in the concentration camp, he established the foundation of logotherapy, which is rooted in the meaning and the power of love. Day after day, hour after hour, his experiences caused an inward peace he had never experienced before.

Nothing in the world can eliminate intentionality in man. The fence of the concentration camp where Frankl once live, the unpierceable walls of jail where St. Paul served his sentence, or the physical disability of Helen Keller--none of these could hold their intention down to the ground. Human intentionality seems to be very fragile but its vitality never shrinks or dies. "Man can preserve a vestige of spiritual freedom, of independence of mind, even in such terrible conditions of psychic and physical stress."[35] This is what Daniel experienced in the lion's cage, what Joseph experienced in slavery, what Peter and Paul and Stephen and many martyrs possessed.

D. Voluntarism

Voluntarism implies the principle of doing something without any external compulsion but with self-generated "will and intention." As a manifestation of human freedom, it is beyond the limit of control by any means, and is fulfilled by man at any cost regardless of the reward or critique. It is, as Carl Rogers defines, a free flowing and autonomous experience toward actualization.[36] Man "moves out voluntarily, freely, responsively, to play his significant part in a world whose determined events move through him and through his spontaneous choice and will.[37]

Gordon Allport's motivation theory explains voluntarism in the different term of functional autonomy--"identical schemata, intentions and generic personal trends" which are instruments for programming.[38] He suggest four principles of Functional Autonomy: First, "contemporaneity" which implies that human autonomous motivation is "now-and-present" goal oriented. It follows from Allport that the terms "now and present" do not necessarily exclude the past and future, but include the impression of the past experience and the projection of the future; that is, the present is not a given consequence of the past, but is potentiality in the making. The goal that the present carries now is impossible without the notion of future. Every contemporary human behavior has an implication for the future, otherwise it is not goal-oriented, nor autonomous. As an example from the political arena, President Nixon's visit to the Republic of China and to the Soviet Union were voluntarily initiated by him, not because of the dangers involved in the present but because of mutual survival in the future. Thus, the present is at the threshold of the future; it is already in the future.

The second principle of "functional autonomy" is "alteration" which implies a continuing growth and change from infancy to maturity. This is a developmental viewpoint of human motivation, which explains voluntary or autonomous motivation to meet "deficiency needs" or "growth needs"--Maslow's notion of "deficiency motivation and growth motivation" respectively. Thus, when a person ceases to exercise his voluntary motivation toward an approximate materialization of infinite potentialities, he has a resigned self and a resigned self is, as Herbert Bonner concludes, a sick self. Voluntary man is on-the-go always, yet (as Eric Fromm implies) the most tragic thing in human life is that voluntary man has to die before he is fully blossomed.

Related to the second principle of "functional autonomy," a third principle is that functional autonomy is the indicant of maturity. In other words, the measurement of description of the level of maturity of a person is made on the basis of the degree of extent and magnitude to which a person exercises his voluntarism--self initiated behavior without external manipulation. The last principle is "individualized difference." Individualized difference implies that a voluntary or autonomous human behavior is manifested differently from person to person because of each person's unique individuality. No two different persons act exactly the same way as the other, although their acts are manifested and observed as though being the same. Thus, individual difference is unaccounted for by behaviorists who hypothetically yet fruitlessly endeavor to manipulate all human behaviors into a comfortably manageable

77

number of classes or categories which are called normalization or standardization. All men are the same under the roof of humanity, and are different under the scrutiny of individuality.

E. Power to Destination

Power as a manifestation of human freedom implies human capability to design, control and modify consequences, in this case, human destination. Namely, power is the maker of human destination, either life or death, and therefore, is actively involved in the making of human destination. Such powerfulness in the exercise of human freedom is not from tradition, legal authority or charisma, as Max Weber writes, but is from the inherent basis of creatureliness of man. It was there when man was created, it is here now in individual man just as it was. It is independent of prescriptions of the crowd, affecting their destinations as well as its own; therefore, as Huxley proclaimed, man is appointed to determine "the future direction of evolution on this earth."[39]

Paul Tillich briefly discusses freedom and destiny in the first volume of his book Systematic Theology. For Tillich, freedom and destiny are in "polar-independence," in which case they are dependent on each other with the process of shaping each other. Without freedom, there is not destiny, and likewise, without destiny, no freedom. Destiny is that out of which freedom arose but arisen freedom shapes destination which in turn becomes the basis of freedom. The intensity of mutuality or polar-independence between freedom and destiny is a measure of power, and its result is observed in the experiential world, in a form of life or death. The power of human freedom, however, further makes man to transcend "life and death" into the world of "free will of God" where man can live in the true freedom. This is where Martin Buber's humanism takes us when he writes that "death and life, so we are told, are only prisons in which we have walled ourselves; we should break them and step forth into freedom where the clearer air showers around us."[40]

Thus, "man is man because he has freedom" and man is the only creature capable of making his own destiny by exercising his freedom.[41] Man is possibly the only creature that knows his destiny: Namely, knows when he is to die and therefore he has his future claimed, and has his future in the planning and in the making. In this way, the power of human freedom holds the future of man, and in turn man holds his uncertain future because of his freedom in power.

Summary

Either negation or sanction of human freedom is the serious choice that every individual human being or human group is faced with as he or any group of people performs activities not only in the academic world but also in ordinary life process. Decision is the energizer of activity, and the foundation of it as well. "Quo vadis" is man's destination, and thus, man is created to be free, and not created to be not free.

For the sake of science, Skinner and his colleagues negate human freedom. But their negation is based on an arbitrary assumption which consequently demands the negation of human freedom unwillingly, and therefore it appears to be unavoidable, what they call "escape." They, however, do not assess the origin of science or scientific method, and the knowledge into which science is rooted for its symbiotic and parasitic survival. They are forced to close their minds in the sacred name of science, and become not capable of appreciating the authentic human testimonies such as "no science without human touch" (Viktor Frankl), or "science lagging behind human inventions" (Charles Frankel), or "scientific knowledge as personal knowledge" (Michael Polanyi) and so on.

Soren Kierkegaard, Jean-Paul Sartre, Paul Tillich, and Herbert Bonner expound the sanction of human freedom. Human freedom is the foundation of all human behavior including the foundation of holy communion between God and man. It is the only human vehicle which unites two into one union (den Enkelte). Furthermore, it is the foundation of human reasoning, whereupon human creativity rises.

According to theology, within the limit of God's free will, human freedom is unlimited and therefore of infinite potential. Thus, man is predestined to be free, and within his freedom he is unpredestined. Man is the manifestation of divinely inherited Logos, since he was created in the image of God, the Logos. God gave man his freedom by virtue of man's capability of knowing good and evil. If man knows only what is good, he is not free to choose good. Man is left free in the world of good and evil wherein to exercise his freedom.

The natures of human freedom are illuminated in characteristics of divine predestination, will to choose, intention, voluntarism, and destination. Human dignity, human creativity, human morality and human proaction are equally important manifestations of human freedom. Incomparable human worth stems from human freedom; human creativity becomes possible within the free exercise of human freedom; without free exercise of human freedom man is not a responsible lover; and man cannot "become" without freedom to be. Thus, human freedom is the essential quality of human nature, and accordingly, human freedom represents authentic humanity. Man as man is in absolute freedom, except he is not free not to be free.[42]

FOOTNOTES

1. Alburey Castell, The Self in Philosophy (New York, 1965), pp. 10-16.

2. See B. F. Skinner, Walden Two (New York, 1962).

3. Skinner, Science and Human Behavior (New York, 1953), p. 315.

4. Ibid., pp. 315-447.

5. Skinner, Beyond Freedom and Dignity, p. 28.

6. Cf. Konard Lorenz, Studies in Animal and Human Behavior, vol. 2, trans. Robert Martin (Cambridge, 1971), pp. 115-146.

7. Skinner, Beyond Freedom and Dignity, p. 28.

8. Ibid., pp. 32-35.

9. Ibid., p. 40.

10. The quotation is from Skinner, Beyond Freedom and Dignity, p. 41.

11. V. Eller, Kierkegaard and Radical Discipleship: A New Perspective (New Jersey, 1968), p. 117.

12. Ibid., p. 119.

13. Ibid., p. 120.

14. See Matt. 12:10-14; Exod. 20:10; Neh. 13:19; and Jer. 17:21.

15. Soren Kierkegaard, Purity of Heart, trans. D. V. Steer (New York, 1948), p. 185.

16. Martin Buber, Between Man and Man (New York, 1970), p. 65.

17. Ibid., p. 52.
18. Jean-Paul Satre, Of Human Freedom, ed. Wade Baskin (New York, 1966), p. 37.

19. Ibid., p. 38.

20. Ibid., pp. 56-93, See also Matt. 10:28-30.

21. Tillich uses his friend professor Durt Riegler's term "man changeable and unchangeable." See Tillich's article, "Human Nature and Change: A Symposium," THe Nature of Man, ed. Simon Doniger (New York, 1962), p. 177.

22. Paul Tillich, Systematic Theology I (Chicago, 1965), pp. 82-91.

23. Ibid., pp. 117-180.

24. Paul Tillich, "Existentialism, Psychotherapy, and the Nature of Man," in The Nature of Man, ed. Doniger, p. 48.

25. Herbert Bonner, On Being Mindful of Man (New York, 1965), pp. 82-91.

26. Ibid., pp. 87-88.

27. Martin Luther says: "...wisdom for Christians to know...For will of God is effective and cannot be hindered...If it (free will) be ascribed into man it is not...properly ascribed...Whereas it becomes theologians to refrain from the use of this term all together..." as quoted in Castell, The Self in Philosophy, pp. 64-65.

28. Satre, On Human Freedom, p. 63.
29. Viktor Frankl, Man's Search for Meaning (New York, 1969), p. 104.

30. Otto Rank, Will Therapy and Truth and Reality, trans. Jessie Taft (New York, 1945), pp. 7-19, 86-97.

31. See Louis H. Bronson, "The Contributions of Virginia Robinson and Jessie Taft to Casework and Practice Theory," mimeographed (School of Social Work, University of Southern California, 1967).

32. Webster's 17th New Collegiate Dictionary, p. 440.

33. Paul Tillich, Courage to Be (New Haven, 1953), p. 84.

34. Frankl, Man's Search, p. 30-93.

35. Ibid., p. 104.

36. Carol R. Rogers, "A Theory of Therapy, Personality, and Interpersonal Relationships, as Developed in the Client-Centered Framework," in _Psychology: A Study of Science_, vol. 3 (New York, 1959), p. 196.

37. Rogers, et.al., _Person to Person_ (New York, 1971), p. 46.

38. See Gordon W. Allport, "Motivation in Personality: Reply to Mr. Bertocci," _Psychological Review_ 47 (Nov. 1940): 545; and "The Open System in Personality Theory," _Journal of Abnormal and Social Psychology_, 61 (1960): 308.

39. Julian Huxley, "Transhumanisn," _Journal of Humanistic Psychology_, 18 (Spring, 1968): 73.

40. Buber, _Between Man and Man_, p. 65.
41. The quotation is from Tillich, _Systematic Theology I_, p. 182.

42. Satre, _On Human Freedom_, p. 37.

Chapter V

THE MORALITY OF MAN

Definition of Morality

A discussion of the morality of man must begin with a definition of "moral." Moral, in Latin "moralis", implies values, principles, consideration, convictions, or conduct with an emotion which is deeply rooted in mind, and therefore is related to the judgement and sanction of either good or bad, right or wrong.

Webster interprets moral as synonymous with "ethical, virtuous, righteous and noble." Ethical implies conformity to a code or to other considerations of right, fair, and equitable conduct; virtuous indicates a blended rectitude and integrity (often it implies abstinence from illicit sex); righteous implies freedom from guilt, culpability, or questionability and may suggest religious or sectarian sanction or sanctimoniousness; noble implies moral eminence with lack of any taint or the petty or dubious—substantiated further by a quote from J. L. Liebman who said, "The true task of man is to create for himself a noble memory, a mind filled with grandeur, forgiveness, restless idols, and dynamic ethical ferment preached by all religions at their best."[1]

The morality of man, or human morality, then, implies man's tendency as well as potential capability, or personality trait, to choose "good's and right's" and to behave accordingly. Such tendency, potential capability or trait of man is universal; every individual man possesses it simply by being a man, and therefore man originally needs no coercion to seek to behave morally. Man wishes to behave morally because morality is one of his intrinsic properties; he knows a moral behavior is humanly desirable and infinitely good and right.

Human morality, as an intrinsic human tendency, potential capability or trait, has its Biblical existence from the time of creation. However, according to the book of Genisis, due to "once-for-all" misexercise of human freedom by Adam and Eve, man had to shamefully fall, and man came to know what shame is (Gen. 2:25) and came to know both good and evil (Gen. 3:5). Although the Creator made man to live in peace and rest without death (Gen. 2), the freedom that He gave to man entailed "freedom" to choose something which man was forbidden to choose, and consequently brought violence, unrest and death to mankind. Thus, immorality as sinful (Gen. 20:6, 39:9) became, in the Biblical inter- pretation, an inherited nature of man, causing human miseries constantly. from the early history of mankind (a universal punishment--Gen. 3:15-24, 4:7), and implanted an eternal human cry of anguish into the heart of man (Ps. 51, Rom. 7:18-20). Moreover, remorse, and repentance, and confession are religious manifestations of human morality, and are what Kierkegaard calls 'Eternity's Emissaries to man.[2]

Human morality is what makes man distinctively human, for H. L. Parsons. Parsons states, "To be truely human, to have mind and personality, is to be united in ties of sympathy and understanding others."[3] His altrustic concept of human morality is revealed in "free giving as having freely received," and further in the attitude of mourning over the death of his fellow men because the death of fellow men diminishes the totality of survivor's moral exercises.

Human morality as an inner nature of man is developed by Abraham Maslow in his psychology of health. He writes:

> This inner nature...seems not to be intrinsically or primarily necessarily evil. The basic need, the basic human emotions and the basic human capacities are on their face either neutral, pre-moral or positively "good." Destruct- iveness, sadism, crulty, malice, etc...seem to be violent reactions against frustration of our intrinsic needs, emotional and capacities....Human nature is not nearly as bad as it has been thought to be...

> Since this inner nature is good or neutral rather than bad, it is best to bring it out and to encourage it rather than suppress it. If it is permitted to guide our life, we grow healthy , fruitful, and happy...

> If this essential core of the person is denied or suppressed, he gets sick sometimes in obvious ways, sometimes in subtle ways, sometimes immediately, sometimes later...

> This inner nature is not strong and overpowering and unmistakable like the instincts of animals. It is weak and delicate and subtle, and easily overcome by habit, cultural pressure, and wrong attitudes toward it...

Even though weak, it rarely disappears in the normal person--perhaps not even in the sick person. Even though denied it persists underground forever pressing for actualization.[4]

What Maslow advocates is human intrinsic conscience rather than Freud's concept of internalized conscience. He employs the word "neutral" or "pre-moral" in the endeavor to avoid "either-or" supposition, either good or evil; but such permanent, intrinsic and good conscience in human nature unfortunately is weak, yet fortunately never resigns itself to stagnation. The worst enemies of the intrinsic conscience of man are discouragement, compulsion, inhibition, oppression, egotism and irresponsibility. However, the intrinsic good conscience of man wins over the enemies simply because of discouragement, inhibition, and oppression are not to exist forever. No morality is mortal, no immorality is immortal. "Man's sense of mutuality and cooperativeness may be suppressed, but as long as man continues to exist, it cannot be destroyed, for these are traits which are part of his protoplasm."[5]

Love in Human Morality

Our hope is too new and too old-
I do not know what worlds remain to us
Were love not transfigured power
And power not staying love.

> Do not protest: "Let love alone rule"
> Can you prove it true?
> But resolve: every morning
> I shall concern myself anew about the boundry
> Between the loved-deed-Yes and the power-deed-No
> And pressing forward honor reality.

We cannot avoid
Using Power,
Cannot escape the compulsion
To afflict the world
So let us, cautious in direction
And mightly in contradiction,
Love Powerfully.[6]

V. S. Goldstein defines love as "the true norm of human existence and the one real solution to the fundamental human predicament," and as personal relationship of an "I" to a "Thou"

86

by becoming wholly receptive to the other.[7] Her Biblical interpretation of love further suggests that love is self-giving without value judgment; demands no merit in the other, no recompense; fully and freely gives without calculations. It is unconditional forgiveness and concern; and "bears all things, believes all things, hopes all things and endures all things" (1 Cor. 13:7).

What are the qualities of "love" that Goldstein defines above? What is the love that every human being today seeks for?

The qualities of love are "agape, epithymia, philia and eros."[8] Agape as a synonym of charity is the quality of self-trascendence which is the determining element and the ultimate source of moral demands (1 Cor. 13:1-3). Some of its manifestations are longsuffering, kindness, absence of envying, boastlessness, selflessness, othermindedness, no evil thinking, and rejoicing in the truth (1 Cor. 13:4-6). Epithymia is the libidinal quality of love, which is revealed in the other love of the opposite sex, and in basic need for survival. Philia is the friendship quality of love, which is revealed in human social activities, including formal and informal clubs, groups, organizations and colleagues, comrades and so on. As epithymia is interpreted as being associated with emotional needs, and philia with social needs, eros is associated with human religious needs. Eros is the mystical quality in the communion of man with God——human need of God's grace.

Thus, love has all four qualities: agape, epithymia, philia and eros. However, human morality is the virtue of agape rather than any other qualities of love. Such agape (love or charity), as elaborated in the Bible, includes the following three subnatures:

(a) Love transcends knowledge. "Knowledge puffeth up, but charity edifieth" (1 Cor. 8:1). This nature of agape does not necessarily imply anti-intellectualism but more strongly implies the danger of knowledge without love. It implies that love is the foundation of all things, the foundation of faith and hope (1 Cor. 13:13, Gal, 5:6)——the basic ingredient of knowledge.

(b) Love is the power to fulfill the law (Matt. 22:38-39, Rom. 13:8) and the foundation of the "law and the prophets" (Matt. 22:40). "The end of the commandment is charity out of pure heart, and of a good conscience, and of faith unfeigned" (1 Tim. 1:5).

87

(c) Love is longsuffering (1 Cor. 13:4). Longsuffering is a nature of God (Exod. 34:6, Rom. 2:4) for the sake of man. Furthermore, it implies no revenge of retaliation but rather wisdom (James 3:17), calmness (Luke 21:12-19), and patience for the sake of peace (1 Cor. 4:6-8, Gal. 5:22).

For Viktor Frankl, "Love is the only way to grasp another human being in the innermost core of his personality."[9] And for Herbert Bonner, "Love is the giving oneself to another... neither a function nor a reaction, but an act of concern, Sorge, or agape."[10] Especially, Bonner contends with the notion of love as a creative relationship, because by giving oneself to another both have a shared common existence. And in this way, an individual man not only gives self to other fellow men, but takes the needs and wants of other men into his being unconditionally, further endeavors to meet the deficiencies in other beings, and consequently brings forth unity rather than fractionated human relationships. Nevertheless, individual belonging to the unity is not an external captivity but an individual freedom. "Love and care are means for the liberation of the human spirit, not for its enslavement." Therefore, to "Love powerfully" implies to let human spirit go, rather than to have it as a personal property. Such nature of agape is Heidegger's Sorge and Bonner's care—the essence of man simply by virtue of his "being-in-the-world."

Furthermore, Bonner includes in agape accountability or responsibility. For Bonner, accountability or responsibility "to the other" implies what he calls "care," but the difference in meaning between care and responsibility is that care is typically spontaneous, while responsibility is a cognitive act —" a moral decision which I make in relation to another individual, an act of conscious choice." Care, however, is rooted in pity and compassion in a form of simple doing, i.e., mother's care of child, which does not involve an act based on the knowledge or rational choice in which responsibility is rooted. Therefore, care cannot be rationalized, but responsibility can.

Additionally, for Bonner, agape includes sacrifice, "the selfless devotion of one person to another. He proclaims that "all love which transcends the exclusive desire for self-fulfillment by the other, is sacrificial," which further implies no concern for one's own comfort, reward, or receiving, but rather for the other's welfare and betterment. Thus, it is an attitude of "one way giving" and an attitude of giving and more giving, yet having a feeling of not giving all beyond his capability of sacrifice. Bonner's sacrifice is Biblical, and the avenue of life rather than a consequential death. It also extends its true implication to "loving enemies," for which human reasoning is far too short for even minimal comprehension. "Self-sacrifice leads us away from self-absorption. It places the other person inside our own life-sphere as a co-equal."

The last nature of agape that Bonner enumerates is faith. The true meaning of Bonner's faith is the unconditional belief in human sanctity and dignity. As Carl Rogers explains, Bonner's faith in man is of man's complete and absolute trustworthiness as well as of man's care, responsibility and sacrifice. For Bonner, "faith strengthens the unifying power of care, responsibility and self-sacrifice." Thus, faith is one of four essences of agape, yet it is the true manifestation of man. Therefore, Bonner's humanism is rooted in agape and his proactive psychology is a psychology of agape. Agape is man's most treasured sentiment. It "moves men and impels men to move mountains, and so moves life on to greater perfectability." Man is in agape and also he himself is agape.

These natures of agape decorate the whole Bible. "For God so loved the world, that he gave his only begotten Son, that whosoever believeth in him should not perish, but have everlasting life" (John 3:16). Jesus as Christ, the incarnated God as the son of man, was born in Bethlehem, lived for the lost, and died on the Cross of Calvary for the salvation of man. When He was with sinful men, He ate with sinners, loved them, taught them with the fullest compassion, which was beyond human reasoning and beyond the reach of man's slow understanding and acceptance. He himself as agape taught sinful men the law to fulfill the laws (Matt. 5:18-19). Throughout the synoptic gospels, Jesus demonstrated agape even to the enemies who tried to crucify Him. He healed Malchus's ear (John 18:10-11) and prayed for the forgiveness of the sinners who crucified Him (Luke 23:34). His suffering was for man, and to complete His agape; He suffered with no revenge or retaliation but with calmness and patience.

His demonstrations of agape are revealed in the lives of His disciples (the Acts of the Apostles) and His followers. Francis of Assisi left his father's home to live among and for the poor; Luther committed himself selflessly for the true message of God; Wesley carried the Gospel to the common folk of England. Puritans, Pilgrims and Friends alike suffered with unspeakable patience for the sake of their belief in agape, the Christ.

In the Old Testament, there are many characters who had lived in the spirit of agape--the selfless leader of the Israelites, Moses (Ecod.); the true friend of David, Jonathan (1 Sam. 18); a woman of tenderness, humility, and purity, the mother of Samuel, Hannah (1 Sam.); the Queen of Sheba, self-committed to her people's welfare, a wife of Solomon, and one who sought for Solomon's wisdom (1 Kings 10); the Shunemmite woman of unselfish endurance in grief and anxiety (2 Kings 4); and many more characters such as Ruth, Esther, Deborah, and so on. The true lesson taught by the people selectively named above is the true nature of the man who is made of love, and they are typical manifestations of human love in man. Man thirsts for love, and to love is man's duty and man's everlasting means to the realization of human potentiality. To "love powerfully" is the commandment of true humanism, and "... love is the ultimate and the highest goal to which man can aspire... The Salvation of man is through love and in love."[11]

Responsibility in Human Morality

Human morality implies a responsible attitude of man, that is, by simply being human an individual man has responsibility for loving fellow human beings and other creatures, and therefore man is capable of being responsible.

Responsibility is personal accounting for one's own acts emanating from the conscious reasoning of the human mind. It is, as Bonner defines it, a cognitive act based on knowledge or rational choice. The individual human being defines his responsibility, and it is also prescribed by the society and culture in which an individual lives. Thus, responsibility is both subjectively imposed and objectively given. When parents accept responsibility to take care of their children, or a teacher or worker extends his working hours beyond the regulated occupational hours, these represent self-imposed responsibility, and the behavior manifests voluntarism and spontaneity on the part of the individual. In this way, self-imposed responsibility implies what "care-Sorge" connoted, but the difference between the two concepts--responsibility and care--is that the former is rooted in reasoning and choice, and the latter is not. The former appeals to knowledge in consciousness, and accordingly is a contingency, while the latter appeals to "itself" and accordingly is independent and absolute. When the responsibility is defined by legal and occupational institutions (objectively given responsibilities) the performance of responsibility as prescribed is not based on voluntarism but on demand. A yearly report on personal income is legitimate, therefore, all working people are responsible for the report in accordance to the legitimate rules and regulations. Another example is that an automobile driver's responsibility to follow the traffic laws is demanded for his welfare as well as that of others.

The definition of responsibility, therefore, is situational, relative and subject to modification, by virtue of differences in jurisdiction, social and cultural prescription, and variety of location. From state to state, some traffic regulations for which every automobile driver is responsible for obedience vary slightly. And also, when an American citizen leaves his country for some reason, such as missionary work or employment abroad, the federal tax regulation, which would be demanded of him otherwise, does not apply to him, but rather a particular tax regulation for which a particular individual is responsible. The definition of responsibility is based on knowledge or rational choice. For example, to commit an actual killing of one's fellowman is subject to judgement, but the judgment is made solely on the basis of the definition of responsibility. The responsibility of soldiers in the battlefield is to fight against an enemy, in which case killing the enemy's men is the given responsibility demanded of every soldier. Moreover, to win the battle, possibly after killing many enemies, is recognized as glory and honor, rather than an irresponsible behavior. In peacetime, or in a territory with no war, however, to kill fellow men with the same weapon that is utilized in the battlefield, is recognized as disgrace and dishonor, and consequently is subject to judgment due to his irresponsibility.

A.   Freedom and Responsibility

Man is not free not to be free, and thus is destined to be free. By virtue of his preordained human freedom, man is accordingly responsible for his conduct which originates from, and is energized by, the exercise of human freedom. As Bonner and Skinner both claim, without such freedom man is not responsible, and human moral behavior is impossible. Skinner says, "If we want to say that people are responsible, we must do nothing to infringe their freedom since if they are not free to act they cannot be held responsible. If we want to say they are free, we must hold them responsible for their behavior by maintaining punitive contingencies..."[12] For Skinner, punitive reinforcement (punishment) is justifiable due to human freedom. Yet, he negates human freedom, and sanctions reinforcement, which consequently raises inconsistencies. He claims that the environment, not the human being, is responsible for the objectional behavior; and accordingly, it is not the attributes of individual human beings which are to be changed, but those of the environment. In this way, Skinner negates human responsibility by blaming environmental attributes as causes of objectional behavior of man. In spite of his assumption that the human being is not responsible for his conduct, he still advocates "scientific control--reinforcement" applied to the process of human behavior modification. At any rate, Skinner claims the mutual necessity of freedom and responsibility, and states that "the responsible person is a 'deserving' person."[13] Martin Buber puts freedom and responsibility together by saying that man is not freed from responsibility. To be moral, man has to be free to make his moral decision. By making a moral decision on his will, man is morally responsible.

B. Guidance and Responsibility

Man acts morally and responsibly. This is a given nature of free man. Why, then, someone would question, do some individuals behave immorally and irresponsibly? The answer is that they have also freedom to choose an immoral behavior based on their miscalculation or emptiness. This does not imply that they are intrinsically immoral or irresponsible people, but implies that they are common ordinary people who have the right to make a wrong choice, and also accordingly that they are absolutely responsible for their immoral behavior. Contemporary criminology is rooted in a philosophical assumption advocating treatment and guidance rather than traditional harsh punishment. This implies that man is made to be moral and responsible, and an immoral and irresponsible behavior is a temporal condition that can be remedied.

Guidance is then needed to uncover the intrinsically responsible nature of man that is temporarily hidden. This, however, does not suggest imposition of some external stimulus upon the person who is known as irresponsible, but suggests a provision of freedom with which the person can test out his responsible behavior and consequently grow into a responsible being. No human responsibility is an empty myth, and when anyone builds a theory or practice upon such a myth, he is committing an irresponsible behavior against a fellow human being. As individual man has a right to believe that he is responsible, in the same right, he also has a duty to believe his fellow men are equally responsible beings. Such an attitude makes mutual trust possible in human relations, and eventually contributes to the maximum realization of infinite human potentiality. This is the true meaning of guidance, not only for irresponsible conducts but even for responsible conducts seeking betterment.

A responsible conduct at times is treated as though it is an irresponsible one, but responsible conduct is immortal. No irresponsible conduct reigns in moral codes forever. A brave military man who fought the Archidamian War against Sparta, Socrates, was respected by young people of Athens.[15] At that time (about 400 B.C.), an unfortunate loss of the war brought a charge by Meletus and Anytus that Socrates had behaved irresponsibly in not worshiping the gods that the State worshiped, and in corrupting the spirit of the youth. Because of the charge, he took a cup of poison. But he was an ordinary man responsible for what he had said and taught. He rejected advoiding the charge by exile, by paying "mina"--a reasonable ransom for war prisoners which was made by the donation from Crito and Plato, and by letting his wife, Xanthippe and infant children cry for redemption. He rejected avoiding the charge simply because of possible nullification of his responsible and uncompromising religious practice and teaching. Socrates' "mysterious voice" did not answer his question, "Am I really wrong, irresponsible?" but rather enriched his life in prison, and he was haunted in the dream of "practice music"--philosophy, the true music. Taylor testifies:

> Socrates owes his immorality of fame as the martyr of philosophy not to any melodramatic outburst of popular sentiment on the part of an emotional democracy, but to the Providence which gave him a younger friend and follower--the one man in history who has combined supreme greatness as a philosophic thinker with equal greatness as a master of language, and so has been, directly or indirectly, the teacher of all thinking men since his own day.[16]

C. Self-Examination and Responsibility

Since human responsibility is situational, relative and subject to modification, man is expected to examine himself in relation to his true responsibility.

O, if I could rightly test myself,
    Then, no one would be judged as I would be;
I shall not rebuke others
    Until I have first judged myself.

93

> Lord, help me test myself still more,
> Because I am very obscure to myself;
> I can judge only on the basis of what I myself am,
> A self fallen into serious judgment.[17]

Consistent self-evaluation of one's responsibility is also a responsibility of man. It is to examine one's individual responsibility in terms of "the mighty responsibility of love for the whole untraceable world-event, for the profound belonging to the world before the Face of God."[18] And such examination, for Kierkegaard, is a purely personal propensity, and must take place before God (1 Cor. 11:28).

The Ten Commandments encompass all moral behaviors for which all men expected to be responsible (Exod. 20). The first four commandments indicate human responsibility toward God, the Maker of man--love toward God; the next six commandments, love toward fellow human beings (Matt. 23:36-39). Briefly, the true responsibility of man is to love--to love God and man. Therefore, with self-examining of one's responsibility, man is responsible to modify his behaviors as he performs the activities of love, and before God man is to search for better ways to love. Thus, human responsibility to love is the means to the completion of love, and consequently brings forth a mutual comprehension of others, a peaceful settlement in the society, and an authentic human fellowship among men. To love is to be responsible for the true responsibility, human loving. Therefore, Hasidism teaches, according to Buber, that:

> Each man has an infinite sphere of responsibility, responsibility before the infinite. He moves, he talks, he looks, and each of his glances causes waves to surge in the happening of the world: he cannot know how strong or how far-reaching. Each man with his being and doing determines the fate of the world in a measure unknowable to him and all others; for the causality which we can perceive is indeed only a tiny segment of the inconceivable, manifold, invisible, working of all upon all. Thus, every human action is a vessel of infinite responsibility.[19]

Avoda (service) and Shiflut (humanity) are two cores of teachings of Hasidism--the nature of human morality.[20] For Buber, Avoda is given to the human spirit and the avenue to Shekina (the prescence of God). It is the service of God and fellowmen in time and space. For Buber, Shiflut is unique in man, and that "uniqueness is the essential good of man that is given to the human to unfold." When it is unfolded, it is

94

revealed in the form of humble man, and humble man is to love, love more—love God and man; namely, humble man loves man and helps fellowmen to love.

Development of Human Morality

Human morality in terms of agape and responsibility is an essence in man, and it is given rather than obtained. Man is made in the self-haunted spirit of agape with the capacity for reasoning. Thus human morality is not added to the nature of man, but is rooted in man and grows as man naturally does. Therefore, man is to be moral, and he knows moral behavior is humanly desirable—knows his moral seed planted in the fertile soul of mind has to be cherished.

Since human morality is not a simple concept but an extremely complicated and controversial construct, it appears to be, in truth, included in the areas of scientific study that call for further scientific sophistication. This implies that since the uniqueness of intrinsic intention of stimulus is beyond scientific measurement, only external stimuli can be studied with respect to the development of human morality. The problem, then, is the amount, kind and strength of external stimuli that influence moral development, as well as the locality and temporality of stimuli.

Despite the research problems involved, there are some theorists who have studied human morality—the nature and growth of morality. David P. Ausubel and H. M. Lynd describe moral conduct in the forms of guilt and shame, as a personal response to external events including transgression and temptation. For Ausubel, guilt is "a special kind of negative self-evaluation which occurs when an individual acknowledges that his behavior is at variance with a given moral value to which he feels obligated to conform"; a self-reaction to the injured conscience, which implies a subjective feeling objectively imposed.[21] In short, guilt is one's judgment on not fulfilling his agape and responsibility, or human morality, and it is associated with objective acknowledgment of his failure. On the contrary, shame is a personal reaction to failure to behave morally, but is not associated with objective acknowledgment as yet, therefore is an internally developed fear of objective acknowledgment. In shame, no other person is aware of the failure of human morality except the one who fails. Thus, guilt and shame are the same in terms of "self-reaction or self-judgment," but by virtue of the presence or absence of

95

objective acknowledgment of failure, shame and guilt connote two different implications.

A. Review on Developmental Theories of Morality

Lawrence Kohlberg contends that morality is the central category for defining social relationship and development of an individual.[22] And further, morality is an internalization of social relationship and cultural rules by the individual, and the internalized morality is called conscience.

Moral development, therefore, for Kohlberg, is conceived of as the increase of such internalization, and the increase of it will simultaneously occur as an individual's social relation and exposure to the culture increase. Thus, moral development will continually occur throughout individual life, but it occurs at different levels of sophistication in accordance with individual age, mentality and physical limitation. However, at any level, three major aspects of internalization should occur in a constant cycling: those aspects of internalization are: (a) the behavioral aspect, (b) the emotional aspect, and (c) the organizational aspect. The behavioral aspect of internalization implies an internally motivated conformity or resistance to temptation. This calls for an endurance and tolerance prior to the external revealment. The emotional aspect of internalization implies self-punitiveness in the form of either shame or guilt, and self-criticism upon the event or thought in terms of its nature of good or bad, right or wrong. The organizational aspect of internalization implies an independent practice of the internalized values which are finalized through behavioral endurance and tolerance, and through self-punishment and self-criticism. It is a finalized standard to maintain one's moral behavior.

Kohlberg concludes, therefore, that moral conduct is in large part nothing but a result of an individual decision in a specific moral conflict situation, and is a general product of development. It increases regularly with age throughout early and middle childhood. Therefore, moral development, for Kohlberg, in terms of internalization process, is in many ways the same regardless of the individual's nationality, social class, peer group or sexuality.

Kohlberg uses Piaget's developmental model of morality. Piaget's developmental theory, as Kohlberg explains, is to suggest that morality is correlated with chronological age, with intelligence controlled ($r=.59$), and additionally to suggest that morality is correlated with intelligence quotient, or I.Q. (r=.31).

For Piaget, as summarized by Kohlberg, there are three levels in moral development: (a) premoral, (b) morality of conventional role conformity, and (c) morality of self-accepted moral principles.[23] The first level would occur during the sensory-motor state; the second during the preoperational stage; and the third during concrete and formal operational stages. However, each level includes two different types of development; namely, in the first level, the child is in "punishment and obedience orientation" (type I) and "Naive instrumental hedonism (type II); in the second level, the child maintains approval from others (type III) and respects authority (type IV); and in the third level, the child maintains contractual morality, individual right and democratically accepted law (type V) and establishes some independent principles of conscience (type VI). In relation to age, level I is in an inverse correlation with age; Level II is in a positive correlation with age up to about the age of thirteen, then no relationship (stablized); and level III is in a positive correlation with age consistently.

Thus, it appears that human morality is a byproduct of human social behavior rather than an unfolding biological and neurological structure of man. Human morality, then, changes with age, and therefore a demand of moral behavior should be contingent upon chronological age and neurological development. Accordingly, it is situational, relative and subject to change. Man is called, however, a moral being not due to his birth into an already established morality but due to his nature, with the unavoidably infinite potentiality to become moral, which eventually makes him different from other creatures in the universe.

Ausubel suggests three developmental stages of human morality which seem to be based on the Freudian concept of superego.[24] The first stage is "assimilation and unconditional acceptance"; namely, the child assimilates parental values and standards, and accepts authority (either from parent or other sources, i.e., other people or institutions) not only due to a consequential reinforcement from not accepting the authority—punishment or anticipation of punishment in the form of pain, deprivation, ridicule and threat, but also due to the maintenance of security and self-esteem. Therefore, this stage, using systems theory, suggests a "hierarchical model"—more power over the other,

$$\frac{dx_1}{dt} = x_1 \quad \frac{dx_2}{dt} = x_1{}^3 + x_1, \ x_1 = x_2 = 1.$$

In the second stage, "the functional stage"—the pre-adolescence and adolescence period, the child begins to lose his volitional dependency upon authority, and develops "a primary status based on his own competency and his equal membership in the social relations." He interprets "rules of conduct as functional to facilitate social organization and interaction rather than as sacred and axiomatic givens." Thus, at this stage, the child develops a concept of "equality of power," which is suggested by systems theory in:

$$\frac{dx_2}{dt} = x_1{}^2 + x_2{}^2 \ ; \ \text{or} \ \frac{dx}{dt} = x_1 x_2.$$

Ausubel's last stage of moral development is "formation of super-ego" which implies that as an individual's constant exposure to a variety of moral standards is made through social interrelationship, the individual can' choose an alternative moral system within the limit, internalizes it as his own moral standard, and practices it independently. This is what systems theory suggests as "limited or unlimited exponential" power:

$$\frac{dt}{dx} = 2x + bx^2 (x(0) = x_o, \ b \ 0), \ \text{or} \ x = \frac{ax_o}{(a+bx_o)e^{-at} - bx_o} \ (\text{limited})$$

and $x = x_o e^{at}$ (unlimited) or $\frac{dx}{dt} = ax; \ x(o) = x_o.$

B. Independent Variables to Moral Development

As revealed in the previous review on the developmental theories of human morality, human morality is highly correlated with age. According to the studies especially done by Kohlberg, Becker, and Piaget, it may be concluded that moral conduct is a gradual product of development.[26] Simple aging process, however, is not the independent variable which contributes to moral development, but the multiplicity and variability of events occurring in the process of aging, such as experience of being punished, experience of commiting transgression, experience of coping with temptations, habit, and so on, all of these are influencing factors upon moral development. Although the findings from studies in regard to the variables contributing to moral development are inconsistent and controversial, some interesting variables controlled in the studies are worthwhile to be reviewed.

Needless to say, Piaget's contention is that the development of individual's intelligence is the most important condition for the development of an individual's morality. But Martha Wolfenstein suggests that warmth, use of love-oriented discipline techniques, and consistency of parental control rather than harsh punishment, facilitate learning of guilt or moral expectation.[27] Whiting, Child, Heinicke and Sears support Becker with a conclusion that "internalized reactions to transgression in the form of guilt, or acceptance of self-responsibility for misdeeds, are more likely to occur when the parent is warm and uses techniques of discipline which utilize the love relations," and "the use of praise and reasoning appears to have the most predictable effects, and love-withdrawing methods seem effective primarily when the parent is high in warmth."[28]

D.W. McKinnon's study on "cheating habit" demonstrated in the behavior of college students reports that a high-cheating behavior is observed among students whose fathers used predominantly physically oppressive forms of punishment, and a low cheating behavior among students whose parents utilized a love-oriented technique. DeVine demonstrates a positive association with use of physical punishment and deprivation of reward, and a negative association with use of reasoning. Sears' findings vary from those of McKinnon and DeVine. Despite such inconsistency in findings, Becker concludes that a power-assertive technique of discipline tends to promote aggression in young children, resistance to authority, power assertion to other children, externalized reaction to transgression, and fear of punishment, projected hostility, while love-oriented technique promotes acceptance of self-responsibility, guilt and internalized reaction to transgression. Additionally he concludes that parent's warmth, model of controlling behavior, verbal reasoning, and timing of punishment termination are equally important.[29]

Burton and Aronson suggest two different conclusions: Burton concludes that there is no positive or consistent relationship between morality and earliness and amount of parental demands, or training in good habits (i.e., obedience, caring for property, neatness, responsibility and honesty), while Aronson concludes that direct training and physical types of punishment may be effective in producing short run situational conformity.[30] Many other scholars suggest various variables which likely influence moral development. Talcott Parsons expands Freud's gratification process between mother and child.[31] George DeVos controls family culture (marriage system).[32] And Else Frenkel-Brunswik controls family system—authoritarian versus egalitarian family.[33] Another interesting study is made by Fred L. Strodtbeck who controls religion as an independent variable to moral development.[34] All studies, however, are yet lacking validation. Future studies are needed, simply because the maturation process of human morality is mysterious. There may be an infinite number of variables that affect moral development. They are therefore, perhaps, beyond human capability of control and comprehension.

Summary

Human morality as intrinsically endowed to the human being upon creation, is humanly potential capability, the tendency to moral behavior which is based on the operation of human mind. It is an essence of man which makes man able to distinguish "good's and right's" from "bad's and wrong's" and to which to behave accordingly. Thus, the human being is destined to be moral, and therefore an immoral man is a "de-natured" human being, not a man.

Biblical teaching reflects human morality. Christian morality and institutional morality are different by the virtue of the difference in moral interpretation. Christian morality interprets moral behavior based on the conative motivation which is beyond public acknowledgement, while institutional interpretation of moral behavior is based on the consequence or the forms of behavioral manifestation. For Christianity, failure to love and irresponsibility are immoral, and immorality is sin.

Although human morality is intrinsic, therefore personal, all moral behaviors bear social implication. This further indicates that there is no personal morality in conflict with social morality, although at times they appear to be in disagreement, since one person can not absorb another's morality. Human morality, however, is to be unfolded even in a harsh trial. And its unfolded manifestations are love and responsibility.

Love has the qualities of agape, epithymia, philia and eros, but human morality is associated with, and rooted in, agape. The nature of agape transcends knowledge and human reasoning, is the avenue to fulfill the law "love of God and man," and is longsuffering with patience. It is loving in giving, and giving more and more, yet one still feels he has not given all but has more to give. Therefore, love is to care, is responsible to care, is sacrificial for care, and is to believe in human sanctity and dignity. And further, loving man lives in the spirit of agape, he is agape.

Human responsibility implies that man is accountable for agape—loving God and fellow men. Self-imposed responsibility and objectively given responsibility are the avenues to fulfill the agape, although they are by nature situational, relative and subject to modification.

To be moral, man has to be free to make his moral decision. No responsibility is defined without human freedom, no human freedom is referred to without the definition of responsibility. Therefore, although moral behavior is desirable behavior, immoral behavior is also possible due to man's freedom to make a wrong choice. Immoral behavior does not imply an intrinsic immoral nature of man, but man's miscalculation and temporary misguidance. For such unfortunate and unwilled consequences, guidance and treatment are instrumental for correcting miscalculation, and developing man's true responsibility in loving God and man is another important responsibility imposed upon man. And in doing so, each man is accordingly responsible to answer the question, "What does God require of me?"

Some research studies imply that human morality is developmental, that human morality is a product of personal cognition and social interaction in which a person actively participates. Therefore, it is highly correlated with chronological age, and accordingly the level of sophistication and expectation of the moral behavior are situational, relative and subject to modification. Human morality, however, is an intrinsic tendency of man with infinite potentiality. It is freely given to man upon creation, and therefore it is man's responsibility to unfold it in his living.

FOOTNOTES

1. J. L. Liebman as quoted in Webster's Third New International Dictionary (1961), p. 1468.

2. Soren Kierkegaard, Purity of Heart, trans. D. V. Steer (New York, 1948), p. 39.

3. H. L. Parsons, "Rooted and Grounded in Love," in The Nature of Man, ed. Simon Doninger (New York, 1962), pp. 78-85.

4. Abraham Maslow, Toward a Psychology of Being (New York, 1968), pp. 2-7.

5. Ashley Montagu, On Being Human (New York, 1951), p. 101.

6. Martin Buber, A Believing Humanism (New York, 1967), p. 45.

7. V. S. Goldstein, "The Human Situation: A Feminine View Point," in The Nature of Man, ed. Doninger, p. 152.

8. Paul Tillich, Morality and Beyond (New York, 1963), pp. 32-42.

9. Viktor Frankl, Man's Search for Meaning (New York, 1969), p. 176.

10. Herbert Bonner, On Being Mindful of Man (New York, 1965), pp. 147-165.

11. Frankl, Man's Search for Meaning, pp. 58-59.

12. B. F. Skinner, Beyond Freedom and Dignity (New York, 1971), p. 73.

13. Ibid., pp. 71-74.

14. Martin Buber, I and Thou, trans. R. G. Smith (New York, 1965), p. 108.

15. Rollins Chamblis, Social Thought (New York, 1954), pp. 158-161.

16. Alfred Edward Taylor, Socrates (New York, 1933), p. 120.

17. V. Eller, Kierkegarrd and Radical Discipleship (New Jersey, 1968), p. 180.

18. Buber, I and Thou, p. 108.

19. Buber, Hasidism and Modern Man, ed. and trans. Maurice Friedman (New York, 1958), pp. 67-68.

20. There are two other cores of the teaching of Hasidism: Hitlahavut (Ecstacy) and Kavana (Intention). See Buber, Hasidism and Modern Man, pp. 72-122.

21. The quotation is from David P. Ausubel, "Relationship between
    Shame and Guilt in the Socialization Process," Psychological Review 62(1955): 379. See, for further definition of guilt, Helen M. Lynd, On Shame and the Search for Identity (New York, 1958), pp. 20-27.

22. Lawrence Kohlberg, "Development of Moral Character and Moral
    Ideology," in Review of Child Development Research, ed. Martin L. Hoffman and Lois W. Hoffman (New York, 1964), pp. 383-384.

23. The original source of Piaget's theory is Jean Piaget, The Moral Judgment of the Child (Glencoe, Ill., 1948). See Kohlberg's, "Development of Moral Character."

24. See Ausubel, "Relationship," pp. 379-380.

25. See, for systems theory, A. D. Hall and R. E. Fagen, "Defin-
    ition of System," in Modern Systems Research for the Behavioral Scientist, ed. Walter Buckly (Chicago, 1969), pp. 89-91.

26. W. C. Becker, "Consequences of Different Kinds of Parental Discipline," in Review of Child Development Research, ed. Martin L. Hoffman and Lois W. Hoffman (New York, 1964), pp. 169-204.

27. Martin Wolfenstein discusses a variation of the forms of punishment in her article, "Some Variants in Moral Training of Children," in Childhood and Contemporary Culture, ed. Margret Mead and Martha Wolfenstein (Chicago, 1958), pp. 249-268.

28. Becker, "Consequences of Different Kinds," pp. 176-189.

29. Ibid.

30. Kohlberg, "Development of Moral Character," pp. 388-389.

31. Talcott Parsons, "The Incest Taboo in Relation to Social Structure and the Socialization of the Child," in Personality and Social Systems, ed. Neil J. Smelser and William T. Smelser (New York, 1965), pp. 136-149.

32. George DeVos, "The Relation of Guilt Toward Parents to Achievement and Arranged Marriage Among the Japanese," in Personality and Social Systems, ed. Smelser and Smelser, pp. 150-167.

33. Else Frenkel-Brunswick, "Differential Patterns of Social Outlook and Personality in Family and Children," in Childhood and Contemporary Culture, ed. Mead and Wolfenstein, pp. 369-404.

34. Fred L. Strodtbeck, "Family Interaction, Values and Achievement," in Talent and Society, ed. David C. McClelland, et. al. (New York, 1958), pp. 135-194.

Chapter VI

THE PROACTION OF MAN

Man cannot approach the divine by reaching beyond
the human: he can approach Him through becoming human.
To become human is what he, this individual man, has
been created for.

- Martin Buber -

Definition of Proaction

Proactive man refers to man in the making, not made; to man
transforming into maximum actualization; to man transcending man's
troublesome predicaments -- finitude, alienation, suffering, and
so on; and to man of hope, not wish.

Proactive man is not static but on-the-go always; namely,
becoming Being. He courageously moves into the uncertain future
to meet his unique problematic life. He knows that he himself
holds the future despite its uncertainty. Man's future is
absolutely man's in the mercy of God. Man's future is not given
but man-made, and accordingly is in the making. Man's future is
man's only arena for demonstration and maximum completion of his
dignity, freedom, creativity and morality.

Combining Martin Heidegger's So-sein and Zu-sein, it follows
that man is Being in the becoming, becoming into Being. This is
the true meaning of man as "open system," "quantum-like jump" and
"incessant change" expounded by C. W. Graves as his theoretical
concepts. According to Graves, man keeps on in the making, making
to reach a higher level of human existence, but a higher level of
existence is never to be achieved yet in the process of achieving.
At the level of higher and higher, of upper and upper, man
experiences "the winds of knowledge and the surging waves of
confidence."[1] But, by the virtue of himself as the maker of
knowledge and confidence, that is, "being mindful"--infinitely
mighty, omnipotent, and omnipresent in his mind--knowledge and
confidence are infinite and beyond human perception, and thus,
they remain an unreachable mystery. Therefore, Saul Alinsky
indicates that human life is a multiple series of means rather
than ends.[2] The idea of Earl C. Kelly's fully functioning

105

person, Carl Roger's integrated self, Abraham Maslow's actualizing self, all alike emphasize the becoming nature of man.

As Martin Buber sees it, man is more, always more, and is to be more always. And as Carl Rogers contends, the "process of healthy living is not a life for the fainthearted. It involves the stretching and growing of becoming more and more of one's potentialities. It involves the courage to be."[3]

Herbert Bonner describes proactive nature of man as not only the unfolding of inherent potentiality but also a creative transformation toward increasing self-affirmation, self-knowledge, self confidence, and self-validation; that is, the powerful urge of individual man to extend himself beyond the inhibiting present prescription, and into a realization of his haunted--undreamed and unseen--reality. A creative transformation is a process of recognition of human inner "potentia," actualizing potentiality, fulfilling his own Being at the level of appropriate maximization. It is not merely a consequence of a set of conditioned or learned responses, but more significantly a mode of conscious action itself directed toward the future, and a mode of conscious action to achieve a higher level of human existence, a high level of self-integration. Man is not enslaved by the second law of thermodynamics, which implies disorganization, elimination of difference and achievement of equilibrium or homeostasis. He is capable of coping with entropy by producing negentropy, by self-transformation.[4]

Bonner's "Tragic Vision" becomes a dilemma of proactive man. Proactive man has a tragic vision--a vision of his future--which can be only envisioned through the eyes of the human mind. Tragic vision does not necessarily refer to "tragic" per se, because eventually that vision will be materialized victoriously in the future of human reality. Yet, Bonner calls it "tragic" by virtue of its revealment at present "as-if" tragic, that is living in extreme anxiety and living in hardships, which appear to be absurd living. It is not anxiety reduction but anxiety enhancement, not hardship avoidance but hardship engagement. Further, tragic vision is the fountain of renaissance, revolution, reformation and adventure, whose paramount meaning is valuable only to human beings.

Only man is able to transcend a troublesome present into the human paradox--tragic vision-- and to unfold himself into it. The mystery of mysteries is that, at present, man lives in the world of his forefathers' paradox and accordingly his offspring will be appreciative with the "as-if paradox" of present man, the dreams yet to be accomplished. As M. Boole says, "We feel as our ancestors thought; as we think, so will our descendents feel."[5] Therefore, human history itself is paradoxical and mysterious; such nature, however, truly is the treasure of mankind and is only a prelude of mystery which is to be in the composing rather than composed. Thus, as Eric Fromm sees it, human life is a process of continuous birth, but the tragedy is that man dies before he is fully born.

It follows that proactive man does not aim for personal happiness but for a continuing self-fulfillment, and values the enhancing and deepening emotions and feelings and the heightening of human sensibilities. In doing so, man is not living with wishes but hopes. "Wish" refers to a personal state in absence of action, expecting something achieved by an external power. It refers to a personal state in which the extent of strength of need (in an object that person wishes for) is much weaker than that in hope. "Hope," on the contrary, is a personal state to achieve, in action, something by himself, not by withdrawing or stagnating but by involving himself in moving forward. Accomplishment of the wishes of wishful man is contingent upon external events, therefore pessimistically dependent; but accomplishment of the hopes of hopeful man is contingent upon internally conscious willing, therefore optimistically independent. Thus, proactive man is not wishful but hopeful.

Infinite Potentiality of Man

Gordon Allport's becoming man does not imply a collection of acts, not simply the locus of acts, but precisely implies that man is the source of acts by virtue of his being mindful.[6] His mind produces infinite multiple-transitional acts beyond human perception, and accordingly maintains potentialities unfulfilled and incompleted at all times.

Then, what really is man infinitely potential for? Is he potential only to be an artist? Or, is he potential only to be an engineer? Is an artist born only to be an artist, or, is an engineer born only to be an engineer? What is the true meaning of the infinite potentiality of man?

The infinite potentiality of man is to become. For Allport, man is less a finished product than a transitive process, and therefore he is continually in the process of undergoing change. "Unlike plants and lower animals, man is not merely a creature of cell structure, tropism, and instinct; he does not live his life by repeating, with trivial variation, the pattern of his species.[7] Allport calls such becoming potentiality of man "infinitely beyond." Such infinite beyondness of human potentiality implies a transcending power in man even beyond his dignity, freedom, creativity, and morality, into the sphere of almighty Thou there to institute and partake of communion. This is what Buber's Hasidism calls "becoming one" in the sight of God, becoming "humanly holy." The infinite potentiality of man implies not to become an occupational expert or a natured talent, but beyond that, to become a fuller being yet becoming more and more beyond the fullest being.

Maslow's psychology of Being is a psychology of human actualization, and is synonymous with Allport's becoming. Therefore human actualization also connotes a never ending process, and thus should be re-worded as actualizing because "ing" discounts "-ed" in actualized, whose meaning is literally included in actualization. Then, man is not in the state of "actualized" but is in the process of "actualizing." Therefore, such a concept of homeostasis—steady or optimum state of an organism—is a distortion of the essence of human "actualizing" and "becoming." Thus, Allport's becoming and Maslow's actualizing both imply the process of maximization of human potentiality. Herbert Bonner puts them together by saying that "becoming is the process of actualizing potentialities, of fulfilling one's own being."[8] Actualization is the process of becoming one's Being, and fulfilling one's own potentiality. Therefore, Bonner says, "man is being in becoming." This unique nature of becoming is the potentiality of man, and is infinite as well as absolute by nature. Again, like any other essential nature of man, man is also to become, he is not made not to become. Thus, the becoming nature of man is the basic attribute of human growth.

Biblically, all men are sinners in the sight of God. Jean-Paul Sartre rationalizes universal sin by saying that man is responsible for his potentiality, yet his responsibility is irresponsibly executed in not making his potentiality materialized as it was originated to be. In other words, materialization of potentiality is impossible for any man, and "sin" is due to potentiality incompleted.

Theologically, man can fulfill his potential only by the grace of God. All things that man possibly can do merely additionally substantiates the maximization of his potentiality. But, at stake is an argument in relation to the source of all things—what brings all things, that is, the teleological causality of human action. Mental or physiological human action is the vessel of the approximately closest distance to human potentiality. Whatever the causality of human action is, however, either external or internal, human action is a consequential revealment of the principle--"structural accomodation-functional assimilation" (Piaget) or "GM-DM" (Maslow); one implies organizational potentiality of man, and another adaptational potentiality. Further potentialities of man are transformation and transcendence.

A. Organizational Potentiality

Organizational potentiality implies human capability of internalizing external phenomena. Such human capability of internalization requires three basic potentialities of man: (a) cognitive potentiality, (b) interpretive potentiality, and (c) independent potentiality. Cognitive potentiality of man includes human ability of storing information imported from his external world to his own internal memory system. It also includes the selectivity of information to fulfill his interpretive potentiality. Interpretive potentiality is an internal process of valuation of available information and process of incorporation of valuation into the stored information, and then, a process of building personal knowledge. Independent potentiality refers to human capability of utilizing personal knowledge in his living. In doing so, man is also fully aware of the fact that he is with other human beings, so that his independent actualization of personal organization or knowledge will not jeopardize his efforts to maximize potentiality. The organizational potentiality of man implies man's capability of organizing himself based on imported information and on his uniquely internal need; that is, to be structurally equipped to accommodate functional demands in reality. Therefore, all men are the same in terms of possessing such infinite potentiality of organization, yet each is differentiated from the other by virtue of infinite differences in their respective potential organization. Such organizational potentiality of man begets human creativity.

B. Adaptational Potentiality

Adaptational potentiality includes human capability of adjusting oneself to the given environment in which he is actively participating. The potentiality of man is more than an ability for survival observed in all species--biological adjustment to the environment. Man positively engages in environmental creation, not due to the fact of his inability to survive in that particular environment but due to his future prospectives of environment. He is not avoiding it but facing it. On the contrary, all other creatures engage passively in environmental change due to the fact that there is nothing they can do to it except avoid it or escape from it. Thus, man only is capable of adjusting himself to the environment and making an environment for human betterment. Man not only possesses such characteristics of open systems as importation of energy, processing of energy, exportation of energy, feedback, negentropy production, equifinality, homeostasis and so on, but also uniquely possesses the character of being a microcosm of the universe. As an example "homeostasis" is not a concept describing human adaptational potentiality. The human organism is more complex and biologically the absolute, the complete one. Man, as well as his organizations (society or social systems), is changing with time, never a static being but rather in a becoming process. Human homeostasis, then is "moving" homeostasis, and "becoming" homeostasis. It could be called "dynamic" homeostasis.[10]

Therefore, the human organism is made in such a way that it can adjust itself to all kinds of environment. When an environment which man has to be in is not acceptable to him, he exercises his infinite adaptational potentiality, which is manifested in an effort to change his environment to fit his particularity.

C. Transformation

Transformation refers to "unfolding human self" into the future in the making--making who individual man is, what he is potential for, and who he is to be. In doing so, man constantly appreciates human values because what man does depends on who man is, who man is depends on what man does, and to make who he is implies who he is to be.

Transformation involves conscious response to the past, active participation in the present, hopeful movement into the future--that is what Bonner calls "triple modes."[11] For Bonner, the past is in the form of private history and memory. Man, however, is not engulfed by his individually unique past, but engages in the productive process of new information added to impression from the past. Certainly, therefore, the past intrudes into the present and into the future of man, and remains in humanity because it is a necessary attribute of human transformation. It stimulates the process of human becoming, rather than making it to stagger or to sink down.

The present is not a mere consequence of the past. It is in the past, yet still in the making--"making-past." It is in the making, yet making in light of the future which is shared with the present already--the present in the future. The present is the platform where transformation is transpired, and bridges the gap between the past and the future. The present unfolds the past into the future. As Bonner explains, the present is in the sphere of human comprehension, for it consists of ongoing events external to human self, and of human sensations, feelings, and perceptions.

Human future is the world of faith. It is yet to come and "endless-coming" from the beyond, beyond the rainbow of eternity. Man lives in such future by incessant transformation until his death takes him "there"--eternal future. In this way, man lives in an incompleted world, the unseen world. Man does not have the slightest glimpse of his future as to what is to be happening, but knows the One who holds the future and to Him man unfolds his anxiety, suffering and hardship. Accordingly, human future is to be in the fullest of hope, and in such hope man transforms into the future. No hope without future, no future without hope. Hope is in the future, the future is of hope. For Bonner, the future is in becoming and beyond human apprehension, yet is the modifier of the past and the maker of the present. "The future is not empty, merely because it is not yet; on the contrary, it is full of possibilities."[12]

Individual human transformation is a mingling process of the person's past, present, and future; yet the goal toward which he is incessantly transforming is hope in the future. All these aspects of the process shall terminate simultaneously at the first note of the funeral march gracefully predestined for him at his death.

> I am only one, but I am one;
> I cannot do everything,
> But I can do something
> What I can do I ought to do,
> And what I ought to do[13]
> By God's grace I will do.

Man ought to transform, that is what he can do by the grace of God.

Transformation, however, is not in the making based on any external imposition, but in the making within the realization of self and fellow men. As Maslow explains, man is not molded or shaped into transformation, or taught to be transformed. The only meaning of external environment to transformation is to permit man or to assist him to fulfill potential transformation into humanness, simply by the virtue of the human potentiality of transformation divinely and biologically given and therefore unchangeable. It is, for Bonner, the process of externalizing one's potentialities; is a difficult process by virtue of its nature of impossible completion; and is a continuous process of facing novelty, uncertainty and ambiguity. "It is not a life, but a living; not a finding, but a seeking...It is not a 'force' or 'drive,' or a similar mechanistic concept, but a holistic process."[14] Abraham J. Heschel supplements by saying that "being human is a novelty--not a mere repetition or extension of the past, but an anticipation of things to come." He continues, "Being human is a surprise, not a foregone conclusion, and every person is disclosure, an example of exclusiveness."[15]

D. Transcendence

Transcendence refers to capability of overcoming given predicaments and of enhancing them toward the goal; namely, human transcendence is human potentiality to overcome human predicaments whatever they are and to enhance them toward human growth. Bonner sees that transcendence and resistance are intimately related, but "resistance refers to the degree of freedom from external social pressures; transcendence means the capacity to transform oneself in the light of personal goals and values...Transcendence is not ordinarily stimulated by an overpowering need for social adjustment, but by the search for adventure and tension."[16] Further, human transcendence refers to human capability of reaching "beyond" rooted in "Christian dogmatics," and "beyond" further implies that "man is more than a mere something endowed with intelligence, has worked itself out with different variations."[17] Thus, the existence of transcending man is set off from that of other creatures, and belongs to the world of creation where man can continue his creativity in freedom as well as preserve other creatures.

Human transcendence for Kierkegaard, as explained by James Daniel Collins, is fundamentally religious and genuinely founded in being.[18] Its epoch spans man's search for eternal happiness, which man eventually reaches only by a free and individual act. Furthermore, it not only is the avenue to human paradox in subjectivity but beautifies human paradox, and then naturally enriches human existence. Therefore, a transcending power of human being is the source of human endurance and tolerance over intrinsically and extrinsically imposed human predicaments. It is the maker of the disciplined mind of man, and the maker of the overwhelmingly haunted experience of man.

Kierkegaard's notion of human transcendence, however, does not imply human isolation by transcendence, but admits unavoidable human identity in finitude, which further implies man's being-in-the-world with other creatures, yet man's being as active participant rather than mere spectator, and man's free engagement in an effort to share his divine nature with God more richly by searching after God. He further explains no transcendence without objects or problematic human predicaments that are over and beyond even human "transcendability," and also explains that the sole purpose of human life is seeking God by transcending himself. Buber describes transcendence as Hitlahavut (Ecstasy) refering to man and God relationship as simple unity and boundlessness. It is further explained with such words as "above"--above nature, time, even thought--to unlock the true meaning of human life.[19] Man is in the reaching not only beyond ordinary and basic conditions of finite rationality, but further beyond human ecstasy and mystery by exercising his uniquely owned transcending power.

Paul Tillich's dialectical philosophy of life (duality of man: I-Thou relationship; being non-being; potentiality-actuality), rooted in dialogue, explains human life as a dynamic, active moment, rather than a static resting in itself; human life as a process of being, courageously moving into the sphere of nonbeing and designing what is "not yet" (the potentiality) into "being" (the actuality); namely, human life is the movement, as Being from potentiality to actuality--that is, "acorn to oak."[20]

According to Tillich, human life, which dynamically confronts nonbeings--such as anxiety, alienation, suffering, death as well as ecstasy, mystery and so on--consists of two different processes of transcendence: (a) horizontal self-transcendence and (b) vertical self-transcendence. Horizontal self-transcendence is an actualizing process of "movement" from potentiality to actuality--a materializing process of human potentiality in time and space. It is by nature in the making in finitude; then, for Tillich, it is "movement from finite actuality." Furthermore, it is manifested in human intention of creativity, which implies man's incessant needs to create, heading toward an approximation of completely perfect human reality. On the contrary, vertical self-transcendence is a movement beyond the finite world in the direction of the "in-finite"--"the transcendence of finitude." It is an ongoing life process of man to materialize the infinite potentialities of man in his haunted reality, which is never reachable but in the reaching. Such "hauntedness" is in the world of personal religion, philosophy, aesthetics, and poetry--the world pregnant with infinite potentialities--therefore, man lives

113

in the boundless world of mind, the world of "complex of opportunities.[21]

Tragic Vision of Man

Tragic vision is the vision of human mind, ultimate yet private, organized through the eyes of mind. It belongs only to the individual human being who holds the vision, therefore it is meaningful only to him. Naturally, then, it lacks social validation, and is beyond objective observation and experimentation. Furthermore, tragic vision is the ultimate goal toward which human transformation and transcendence proceed, and therefore it is noble and reverent for human life--the life of fully matured, dignified communion between being and non-being; the life of nobility, beauty, authenticity and hope.

Tragic vision further includes in its definition the mind liberated from prejudice, responding to the life of mystery--the mind in deeper sense of humanity. It, however, is not a cheap religiosity but a source of mitigating human despairs and enduring with them. Moreover, it is beyond absurdity, transcending into the actual world of person where the person himself might blossom in the fullest potentiality.

Tragic vision is, for Abraham J. Heschel, "transcendent meaning," a meaning that surpasses absorption, clarity, analysis and comprehension--not finite meaning which is subject to categorization, but infinite meaning.[22] Infinite meaning implies a thought that comprehends the man, and a thought that man encounters. It has depth and quality only manifested in human awe; and it is uncomfortable, not compatible, not to be grasped. It is not an object--not a self-subsistent, timeless idea or value--yet it is a present. It is the premise of wonder (beyond what is given) and the premise of awe--therefore, is not an object of possession, yet man can relate himself to it and be actively engaged in it.

Paul Tillich and Herbert Bonner explain human conditions in different terms: "courage to be" (Tillich) and "human predicament" (Bonner).[23] For Tillich, courage is an ethical human reality rooted in the whole breadth of human existence and the ultimate structure of being. Human courage-to-be is synonymous with human anxiety--"anxiety as the normal state of mind"--courage in anxiety. He explains further three different kinds of anxiety, or three different forms of courage: (a) anxiety of fate; (b) anxiety of meaninglessness; and (c) anxiety of condemnation (guilt feeling).

Bonner's notion of human predicament includes (a) man's finitude; (b) anguish and despair; (c) alienation; and (d) existential guilt. Then, when we combine both Tillich's "courage-to-be" and Bonner's "human predicament," it may be concluded that human conditions are (a) finitude (anxiety of fate, man's finitude); (b) alienation (anxiety of meaninglessness, anguish, and despair); and (c) suffering (anxiety of condemnation and existential guilt). These three are the conditions of modern man which call for imminent tragic vision.

A. Finitude

Human finitude, for Tillich, is a threat to ontic nature of man; namely, a threat to the basic self-affirmation of a being in its simple existence, by virtue of the nature of human finitude being most basic, completely universal and inescapable.

Despite the divine endowment of freedom to man, for Bonner, "modern man is moved far less by his capacity to choose than by his awareness of his own finitude." The reasons are indicated by Bonner. One is the overwhelming, immediate fact of ruthlessness and life destroying power--war and arbitrary limit on human exercise of freedom; and another is the overwhelming impact of science and technology on man's image of himself--an influence of scientism making man devalued so that he consequently loses his confidence in his capacity to direct his own destiny.

Proactive man of tragic vision, however, is not escaping from such helplessness, but courageously and therefore anxiously facing the finitude with the fullest awareness of finitude and with his potentiality for transforming and transcending intention into action. Thus, man sees his finitude as "infinite" until he has to face his own death personally. Yet, the Bible reads, "O, death, where is thy sting? O, grave, where is thy victory? (1 Cor. 15:55). "Death is swallowed up in victory." (1 Cor. 15:54). And Bonner poetically says, "in the lonely moments when a man fearfully waits for the death of a loved one, he becomes so close to life, that life itself becomes tragically meaningful." Death is cutting loose from life--the threshold of eternal living. He concludes "Interest in death is a sign of morbidity."[24]

B. Alienation

Human participation in human relations is a human finitude. By being in the world, man participates in human creativity even if in very small ways, affirming himself as receiving and

115

transforming reality creatively, which eventually results in spiritual creativity, as Tillich explains. Unfortunately, however, such spiritual creativity of modern man is trans-appeared in the form of emptiness and meaninglessness, and finally it has lost the ultimate concern for fulfilling man's divine responsibility as the host of the universe. "Everything is tried, nothing satisfies," says Tillich, and thus, there is no contentment today except man's estrangement, alienation.

As Bonner indicates, the reasons for human immobility are cybernation, and totalization and standardization of the human intellect--effective causes of the depersonalization of modern human life. This depersonalization in turn is the major source of much of the human alienation that agonizes the minds of modern man. Then, we question, "What does alienation imply?"

The term alienation is from the Latin, "alienus, alius," meaning "another." Webster defines it as "strange, different, incongruous, owing different allegiance"; "properly, therefore, belonging to another"; "not of our type." Statistically, alienation is synonymous with "deviation," a tendency or degree which deviates or varies from the average mean. When we apply this analogy to an agricultural experiment, we should describe the stalk of corn that is exceptionally short as deviated from average corn stalks. Thus, we further can expand this analogy to describe anything that differs from what is most common, as deviated, or alienated. Namely, alienation is referred to in medicine essentially as a pathological revealment in the form of a disease or organic dysfunctioning; in sociology, alienation is individual failure in social participation. Whatever definition of alienation is used, however, each definition raises a question: "Who is being alienated from what?" and "Who defines that a particular individual is alienated?"--which eventually leads to an endless and fruitless argument.

"Strangeness" in an individual man is also a byproduct of his nature, uniquely different individuality. Such a unique person is unfortunately seen as strange or different simply because he can never be a subject for a description based on such principles as average, commonality, or even normality. He is "un-alienated" in his lebenswelt from the depth of his mind. Namely, he may be different from an external sophistication but not from self-validation. He may behave differently, but his different behavior is decided upon by subjective interpretation and definition. Human internal suffering, therefore, is a consequence of man's courageous negation of externally imposed coercion, prejudice and ignorance.

116

C. Suffering

Human suffering, as explained by Tillich, originates from human morality, especially man's responsibility to his Beingness. Man's being, for Tillich, is not only given to a human being but also demanded of him--he is responsible for it. Although human finitude defines finite human freedom, man is demanded to become what he is to be. As Tillich says, "man as finite freedom, is free within the contingencies of his finitude." And he continues "within these limits, he (man) is asked to make of himself what he is supposed to become to fulfill his destiny."[25] Then, human suffering is an unavoidable essence of man.

For Bonner, human suffering originates in man's incessant trial to fulfill his unachievable responsibility to love. Namely, human suffering is a consequence of human endeavor to reduce the extent of his existential guilt from not loving fellow human beings, or to completely eliminate such existential guilt. Existential guilt of man is unavoidable because "no one truly loves any one," and therefore, such guilt is "a state of being that is owned" by man. Thus, man joins in suffering, suffering becomes man. Man is suffering.

For proactive man, however, human suffering connotes some existential values which are to be fulfilled through human suffering. In other words, human suffering fills the feeling of emptiness, and maximizes true meaning of human existence. Therefore, individual man claims his share of suffering to grow into a man in the making.

Ralph W. Sockman offers a Biblical interpretation of the values of human suffering, in his book "The Meaning of Suffering." For Sockman, the values of human suffering are discipline, growth, resourcefulness, understanding, assurance and helpfulness.[26]

(1) Discipline. Sockman asks, "Why does a good God permit pain and evil in the world?" and answers, "He does it for the good of His children". Further he adds that "without some hardships and dangers and troubles, life would not seem good to us"--God disciplines him whom He loves most. He cites further Heb. 11:11, "For the moment all discipline seems painful rather than pleasant; later it yields the peaceful fruit of righteousness to those who have been trained by it." In other words, that which compels self-control also liberates the soul.

Although the causes of human suffering are beyond human comprehension by virtue of the enormity of God's universe and the

117

depth of God's love, human troubles are, for Sockman, brought forth by man's carelessness, cruelty and misuse of freedom. The Biblical example of such suffering is Moses' impulsive anger that brought the death of one Egyptian and that consequently led him to a life of hardship as a tender of flocks in Midian (Exod. 2-3). However, his trial and frustration also brought him wisdom and courage to lead the Israelites out of Egypt to Canaan. Therefore, Sockman concludes, "If we are concerned in self, then trouble only makes us feel humiliated...But if we are really God-centered rather than self-centered, then trouble serves to humble us and make us more teachable."

(2) Growth. For Sockman, a process of normal development is a sequence of suffering--that is, no walking without some fallings which bring pains. The fall hurts him, yet despite it he grows--"there are times when it hurts to grow." Even a man Jesus, the Christ, learned obedience through what he suffered (Heb. 5:8) and such process of growing was beyond His parents' understanding (Luke 2:48-49), and led Him to go to Jerusalem to suffer many things (Matt. 16:22), even death. He has overcome the world (John 16:33) through suffering, and become the Lily of the Valley in glory.

(3) Resourcefulness. Suffering is the source of rest, compassion, faith and love. Sockman says, "If our world contained no pain to prick our ease, no suffering to call forth our compassion, no inexplicable sorrows to accept in faith and love; if our days were all sunshine, our lives would become a desert, our streams of sympathy would dry up, our eyes would become spiritually blind and our natures swinishly selfish."[27]

Human suffering is not only the source of human endurance and tolerance over human predicaments, making man noble and strong, but also the spark awakening human talents and responsibilities. Sockman quotes Beethoven's remark of a singer, which reads, "She is a magnificent singer, and yet there's just something lacking in her singing. Life has been too kind to her. But if one day it happened that some one broke her heart, she would be the finest singer in Europe." That is it--human suffering--the mother of true aesthetics. Without actual experience in pain, no one can interpret deep and tender human emotions. A good experience is defined after a bad experience, just as the taste of sweet becomes more cognitive to a person who experienced the taste of bitter tartness. Therefore the apostle Paul says, "When I am weak, then I am strong" (2 Cor. 12:10). We have a hope in the fuller maturity because we know that we are premature. Thus, human suffering is the basic ingredient of the tar on the road to fuller maturation. As Goethe expressed it, "I never had an affliction that I did not turn into a poem"; and in the same attitude, the poet Heine wrote, "out of my deepest sorrows, I make my little songs."[28] Human suffering is the everlastingly over-flowing fountain of human potentialities--which is human mind. Therefore, human mind is in suffering, suffering is in human mind--human mind is human suffering.

(4) Understanding. Sockman's notion of "understanding" is related to human understanding of God as well as a more sympathetic understanding of fellow men. By a break in the family circle, a human individual is reminded of "the love which flowed so steadily through the household that it was taken for granted without gratitude." And also, in tribulation, distress, persecution, famine, nakedness, peril, or sword, man knows that he is more than a conquerer through Christ who loves him (Rom. 8:35-37).

In the process of daily living, primarily occupied by material things, man can, for Sockman, disengage from such ordinary process, and humbly re-engage in "the things that are unseen and eternal." Thus, man preserves his image of God and enriches the process of spiritual life.

(5) Assurance. The apostle Paul's comforting assurance in suffering reads, "We rejoice in our sufferings, knowing that suffering produces endurance, and endurance produces character, and character produces hope, and hope does not disappoint us because God's love has been poured into our hearts through the Holy Spirit which has been given to us" (Rom. 5:3-5). This is a Christian assurance believing in an "unseen" and secret mystery. Tillich explains human suffering as the door to the depth of truth, as a teacher and a purifier. For Tillich, "God brings men into deep waters, not to drown them, but to cleanse them."[29]

(6) Helpfulness. According to Sockman, human suffering is helpful in the process of human transformation into a noble humanity. He interprets the life of Abraham Lincoln in the form of sequential human tragedies which helped him become "the most beloved and inspiring son America has produced."

For a feverish child, a mother suffers to ease the child's discomfort, which implies that one suffers for another in order to ease the other's pain. Moreover, as Sockman explains, by embracing a suffering child, "in our imagination we can think of our heavenly Father with his Everlasting arms of mercy." Thus, by suffering, man is helped to become aware of the eternal love and consequently to become a child of God.

SUMMARY

The proaction of man can be summarized by examples taken from the Bible. Most, if not all, Biblical characters testify that human life is a life of future: man lives in present toward the future, not in the past. Man stands by himself regardless of the recorded specificity of his past, and performs his part in the "play of becoming", becoming into Being. Among the numerous men and women of the Bible who lived "in the future," are Abraham and Joseph.

Abraham lived for tomorrow, completely trusting in the Lord. "By faith Abraham, when he was called to go out into a place which he should after receive for an inheritance, obeyed: and he went out, not knowing whither he went" (Heb. 11:8). Thus, the man of tomorrow goes. Abraham left his well-adjusted surroundings for an unseen, unknown, therefore uncertain future, but he was certain that he would reach such invisible higher ground, the land of promise. Thus, he moved out of a security of yesterday into the devotion of his future, to be made and in the making.

Jacob dreamed great dreams, dreams of the future to come. He was not content, as his brother Esau was, with material abundance, but wanted something else—the spiritual privilege, the birthright, and the chance of achievement and leadership, all of which were "unseen potentialities," only to be materialized in future reality. Would his dreams come true? Indeed they did. They were completed by the life of Joseph who also dreamed of future, and lived in the future. He lived through darkness and hardship in the palace of Pharaoh, yet he was always haunted by the dreams of future. "Behold, this dreamer cometh," said Joseph's brethren. As Joseph, so was Moses; so was Amos the prophet, the unknown and obscure shepherd of Tekoa; and so was the most winsome figure in the history of Israel, David, who dreamed of a fight with Goliath of Gath. All alike dreamed great dreams of the future.

Such man of future is called "proactive man"—man in the becoming "more," more to the most, and beyond the most. He is man of sorrow, haunted with undreamed dreams yet to be accomplished, and also tirelessly unfolding his infinite potentialities in finitude. Thus, proactive man is man of potentiality, potentiality to become. Such potential becoming is enhanced by (a) organizational potentiality, (b) adaptational potentiality,

(c) transformation, and (d) human power of transcendence, "transcendability."

The life of Biblical characters is marked by their owning of tragic vision--"man of tragic vision." Tragic vision is a vision of human mind, therefore, it is noble and reverent. It is a vision of future, vision of human finitude, vision of human distress, alienation and suffering. Such Biblical characters who lived with tragic vision are also too many to be cited. A few were women: Sarah who lived with patience for the promised son Isaac; Jochebed of faith (the immortal mother of Israel), who gave birth to Aaron (a priest and the founder of the Hebrew Priesthood), Miriam (a leader of Israelites) and Moses; Mary, mother of Jesus; and Elisabeth, a mother of John the Baptist, who lived in the unseen world of promise assured by the Angel Gabriel.

The man of tragic vision deeply appreciates the true values of human suffering. A Biblical perspective of the true values of human suffering are enumerated by Sockman: they are (a) discipline, (b) growth, (c) resourcefulness, (d) understanding, (e) assurance, and (f) helpfulness.

Thus, the host of infinite potentiality and tragic vision is called the man. This man is to become, become more, over and beyond the most. Therefore, he lives in present reality, yet in the present realm of haunted future which is in the making, making with an assistance of only humanly unique tragic vision. Tragic vision of man is not an empty religiosity but the divinely instituted and freely yet mercifully given potentiality of humanity.

Herbert Bonner lists the following conditions of tragic vision.[30] (a) _Personal Truth_: Tragic vision suggests personal truth, yet not absolute, not abstract only, but a personal approach to personal knowledge of the vision of mind. (b) _Estrangement_: By virtue of individual uniqueness, each individual man is strange to another, yet without others he is nothing. The individual man of such paradoxical position is self-sufficient, yet dependent on others to validate his existence. Being alone, individual man creates meanings which are not empirical quantity but rather poetic, aesthetic quality; and being with others, he seeks for objective appreciation of his created meanings. Such quality of estranged man, says Buber, is "holy insecurity." (c) _Nothingness and Despair_: For Bonner, scientific experimentation brings man to a contingent nature, and further creates human crisis against which no man has capability of defense. Man endeavors to resolve such crisis, nothingness, emptiness and despair, through personal faith, "courage to be." (d) <u>Solitude</u>: Solitude or loneliness of man implies disengagement of one from another, yet interdependent individuality--somewhat aesthetic individual duality, yet the basic tendency of man. (e) <u>Temporality</u>: Subjective time of human being is phenomenal "lebenswelt" (lived experience), which is either faster or slower than physicist's time. What the individual does now is most clear to him, and what he does now is the projection of his future. Human future molds present experience, and is not empty to the person in the planning of the future, which already is in the present reality. (f) <u>Historicity</u>: History of tragic vision is different from a history which records time. It is a subjectively structured form, uncovered yet alive in the human mind, constantly in the making of individual heritage--heritage "to know how to love" in Kierkegaard's term. (g) <u>Death</u>: Death is the ultimate fate of each human being and a present contemplation of it is a responsibility of self-conscious man. The enhancement of individual death is to be accomplished by the fear of death, but to compel oneself to serve the supreme meaning that he has been searching for and creating. (h) <u>Mobility</u>: Mobility, the last condition of tragic vision, is not pathology but the sign of healthy man. Until the death of man ends human mobility toward making future, man is always to be more, on-the-go. Thus, a proactive man seems to be alone, but never be lonely.

FOOTNOTES

1. C.W. Graves, "Levels of Existence: An Open Systems Theory of Values," Journal of Humanistic Psychology 10(Fall, 1979):132.

2. Saul, D. Alinsky, Reveille for Radicals (Chicago, 1946), pp. 65-74.

3. National Educational Association, Perceiving, Behaving, Becoming (Washington, 1962), p. 52.

4. See Herbert Bonner, On Being Mindful of Man (New York, 1965), pp. 131-146.

5. Boole is quoted in Charlotte Towle, The Learner in Education for the Profession as Seen in Education for Social Work (Chicago, 1954), p. 230.

6. Gordon Allport, Becoming (New Haven, 1966), p. 12.

7. Ibid., pp. 19-22.

8. Bonner, On Being Mindful of Man, p. 141. See also Romans, Chapter 7.

9. Ibid., pp. 131-146, 181-201.

10. See Esther Barnhart (McBride), "A Re-evaluation of Assumptions Commonly Held about Changing Societies" (Paper presented in a graduate course in sociology at Tulane University, New Orleans, Jan. 1966).

11. Bonner, On Being Mindful of Man, p. 118.

12. Ibid., p. 138.

13. Author is unknown. See Romans, Chapter 7.

14. Bonner, On Being Mindful of Man, pp. 142-145.

15. Abraham J. Heschel, Who is Man (Stanford, 1966), p. 37.

16. Bonner, On Being Mindful of Man, pp. 190-191.

17. Martin Heidegger, Being and Time, trans.J. Mac Quarrie and E. Robinson (New York, 1962), p. 72.

18. James Daniel Collins, _The Mind of Kierkegaard_ (Chicago, 1953), p. 159.

19. Heidegger, _On Being and Time_, pp. 74-77.

20. Guyton B. Hammond, _The Power of Self-Transcendence: An Introduction to Philosophical Theology of Paul Tillich_ (St. Louis, 1966), pp. 35-44.

21. Heschel, _Who is Man_, p. 39.

22. _Ibid._, p. 76.

23. See Paul Tillich _Courage To Be_ (New Haven, 1953), pp. 1-85; and Bonner, _On Being Mindful of Man_, pp. 61-80.

24. Bonner, _On Being Mindful of Man_, p. 75.

25. Paul Tillich, _Systematic Theology I_ (Chicago, 1965), pp. 192-200.

26. Ralph W. Sockman, _The Meaning of Suffering_ (New York, 1961), pp. 66-92.

27. _Ibid._, p. 78.

28. _Ibid._, p. 83.

29. The original source of Tillich's explanation of human suffering is Paul Tillich, _The Shaking of the Foundations_ (New York, 1950), pp. 52-59.

30. The conditions of tragic vision are summarized from Herbert Bonner's lecture at California Western University, San Diego, California, Spring 1970.

POSTFACE

Summary: Who Man Is

A clear concept of man defining "who man is" should be the foundation of any profession purporting to serve human beings, professions such as education, medicine, nursing, social work, religion and so on. This is because the nature and process of the services provided by such professions are contingent upon how their professional constituents (and also the human beings served) view man--the man whom they serve for his betterment and consequent welfare.

Through time, the human mind has entertained many different concepts of man. It once lived with "man of survival competition" and "man of mechanistic totality"--the concept of man that prevailed throughout the 1800s. In about the late 1800s and early 1900s, the prevailing view of man became "man of animal" and "man of libido," which are respectively known as the first and second forces in psychology.

Among the less widely accepted views of man developed in the eighteenth and nineteenth centuries was the Leibnitzian school of psychology believing in man as purposive, intellectual, righteous and rational. The vital seeds of the Leibnitzian school have remained intact, even if obscure, and seem to be blossoming in the late twentieth century humanistic views of man. The coming of man would seem to be "man of humanism."

This study of man is an effort to explore the philosophical and religious sources of the humanistic view of man and to review various delineations of "man of humanism." It does not attempt to challenge other concepts of man which have historically prevailed over time, but to supplement them with a humanistic or democratic concept of man in order that as a consequence we might have a better total concept of man. In doing so, this study is rooted in Biblical and humanistic philosophy and humanistic psychology. It eventually deals with the problems of "WHO MAN IS" rather than the more widely studied problem of "WHAT MAN IS." "What man is" concerns human existences, within the realm of verifiable human objectivity. "Who man is" goes beyond human objectivity to encompass human essences, or the genuinely divine natures of man, such as dignity, creativity, freedom, morality and proaction.

125

First, it is perceived that man is created in dignity, the highest quality beyond comparison, solely unique and personal only to man. Such dignity of man originates from man's being created in the image of the Creator, being able to have communion with Him, accordingly being righteous and holy, and possessing humanity—the combination of "animality and angelness" or "imago and similitudo." Unfortunately, the Bible records that man of such omnipotent Being and "once-for-all" fall by rebelling against his Creator, becoming the eternal sinner, and consequently was disqualified for dwelling in the Garden of Eden.

Being a sinner, yet created in the Divine image, man is the only object of divine mercy and grace, and is the potential recipient of salvation and blessings. Even though above any other creature in the universe, man still does not deserve any divine endowments, but these are given to man freely because of God's divine love toward man.

Thus, man possessing the invaluable quality of dignity as his essence, is beautiful—whatever he is—because he is who he is. Man is righteous and holy, because he is created to be so. And man is the unconditional receiver of what he does not deserve. He is dignified, and he owns his eternal dignity.

Secondly, it is perceived that man possesses creativity, the ability to create something out of nothing (product) and to imagine, think, puzzle and so on (process). This creativity makes man human in fullness of mind that initiates creativity infinite in quality and quantity.

Being mindful, the incarnated Logos, man is by nature creative and therefore creativity is his potential destination. Moreover, whatever the creative product or process is, human creativity is an enduring mystery in the universe. Such creativity is further mysteriously communicable from one mind to another and powerfully grows over time. Such mind-to-mind communication and powerful growth make human creativity independent of, and beyond, valuation—subject not to evaluative judgment or objectivity, but to human appreciation and unconditional gratitude.

Human creativity is to grow in accordance with the biological and neurological development of the individual human being. A measure of growth of such ability to create, however, is beyond human comprehension, although slight changes in ability might be speculated from creative products and processes of the individual. The genuine creativity is "there" as human essence regardless of the existential characteristics of the individual and it is rightfully and dutifully in the maximum making of unique potentiality.

Thirdly, it is also perceived that man is created in freedom, and therefore he is free--so free that he can make a wrong choice. It is indicated that man is not free not to be free--man is destined to be free. Such man is born to be capable of exercising his infinite freedom within finitudes to which he is also subject.

The characteristics of human freedom are divine predestination, will to choose, intention, voluntarism and destination (namely, the matter of life or death), and all these characteristics of human freedom are the maker and energizer of human activity regardless of what the activity is. By virtue of these characteristics, human existence as what he is becomes realistically possible, and human existence as what he is to be promises to become reality.

Fourthly, it is perceived that man possesses morality and therefore is potentially trustworthy. Human morality is a human tendency and potential capability of moral behavior based on a judgment of "right or wrong," or "good or bad."

By virtue of possessing morality, man wishes to behave morally. Human immorality manifested in an immoral behavior, however, is a consequence of man's absolute freedom, where he chooses a wrong alternative due to momentary misguidance or miscalculation. Such immorality is not an essence of man, but a byproduct of the human predicament of being not free not to be free.

Being moral, man is lovable and intrinsically "loving"--loving his Creator as well as his fellow men and other creatures. "Being moral" implies that man is agape. Being moral, man is responsible for loving, which is to exercise the nature of agape.

And lastly, it is perceived that man is not a static being but in the process of incessant becoming--becoming who he is to be, and what he is to be--human proaction. Man is to become regardless of his environmental "givens." Although man is to die, up until his glorious moment of death labor, he is to become by unfolding his potentiality, and he reaches toward the closest approximation of his potentiality with assistance from the power of organization, adaptation, transformation and transcendence.

Man in becoming always has tragic vision, the vision of human mind--the vision that enriches human life despite his predicaments of finitude, alienation and suffering. Man has this vision not to escape from, or to surrender to, human predicaments, but to courageously face them and further to enhance his becoming process. Thus, man dreams through this vision, and therefore man is an eternal dreamer in the process of becoming--becoming always to be more, always to be most and always to be beyond the most.

In conclusion, then, all men universally possess the essences of man: dignity, creativity, freedom, morality and proaction. They are "there" at the time of creation and are to be "there" toward infinite eternity. Such essences are what men are about to re-discover today as they design for both the present and the future in the making. These essences are the qualities which bring forth quantities to be evaluated within human objectivity, and therefore they are "there" always and are always to be precious regardless of any degree of quantitative objectivity.

What professionals in human services should concern themselves with are the infinite and intrinsic essences of man, as well as the finite of resultant existences of man. The essences are permanent, absolute and total, while the existences are temporary, relative and fragmental. "Which shall we choose"? is our professional predicament, yet we must choose not "either-or" but "both," for we, being men, are "two-in-one" and yet able to cope with the contrasting "one-in-two." For a consolidated and complete professional foundation--the concept of man-we choose of man--we choose "both," not "either-or"-both human essences and existences.

Debt Shall Be Paid

In approximately 400 B.C., Socrates was sentenced to death on the charge of corrupting the youth of Athens with his philosophical probing and questioning. We, of course, have no way to know how he manipulated the youth in his days to be corrupted, but at any rate, he was compelled to take a cup of poison to die. He was a great teacher and philosopher whose teaching still freshly echoes in the hearts of students (young or old learners)-"Know Thyself," which implies "to know who man really is and what human being is potential for." At the end of his life's journey, he refused to have passionate measures seeking for redemption--cry of survivals or paying ransom money-but courageously accepted a peaceful death labor.

128

Feeling his body to be cold and stiff, he said, "When poison reaches the heart, that will be the end." Then, uncovering his face to Crito, he said, "Crito, I owe a cock to Asclepius. Will you remember to pay the debt?"[1]

Public or private organizations for human services are the arena of human loving-enriching human loving through an exercise of love among constituents (professionals and consumers). By virtue of such loving to be exercised, all constituents of organizations for human services have a "debt to one another"-the debt of loving.

What is to be loving, as it appears in the Biblical work "charity?"

> Charity suffereth long, and is kind; charity envieth not; charity vaunteth not itself, is not puffed up,
>
> Doth not behave itself unseemly, seeketh not her own, is not easily provoked, thinketh no evil;
>
> Rejoiceth not in iniquity, but rejoiceth in the truth;
>
> Beareth all things, believeth all things, hopeth all things, endureth all things.   (I Cor. 13:4-7)

For Rene Descartes, "I think therefore I am," and for Herbert H. Aptekar, "I do, therefore I am a professional."[2] Now, for the man of today and tomorrow, "I love, therefore I am." The debt of love shall be paid off only by loving one another powerfully. Professionals in human services owe more debt of love to the man whom they serve, than any other occupation. Therefore, they are expected to love even more and more powerfully. Loving is the life blood of a human profession.

Let it be said, therefore, "we love, therefore we are professional." Let it be said also, in conclusion, "Think creatively, Do responsibly, and Love powerfully." This is the motto of professionals in human services who committ their careers to practice for the human betterment of today and tomorrow.

BIBLIOGRAPHY

Books

Alinsky, Saul D. Reveille for Radicals. Chicago: University of
Chicago Press, 1946.

Allport, Gordon W. Becoming. New Haven: Yale University Press,
1966.

_____. The Person in Psychology. Boston: Beacon Press,
1968.

Anderson, Harold H., ed. Creativity and Its Cultivation. New
York: Harper and Brothers, 1959.

Barrett, William. What is Existentialism. New York: Grove
Press, 1965.

Blumer, Herbert. Symbolic Interactionism: Perspective and
Method. Englewood Cliffs: Prentice Hall, 1969.

Bonner, Herbert. Psychology and Personality. New York: Ronald
Press Co., 1961.

_____. On Being Mindful of Man. New York: Simon and
Schuster, 1967.

Bowie, Walter Russell. Great Men of the Bible. New York: Harper
and Brothers, 1937.

Brentano, Frances, ed. Nation Under God. New York: Channel
Press, 1964.

Bronowski, J. Science and Human Value. New York: Harper
Torchbooks, 1965.

Buber, Martin. I and Thou. Translated by R.G. Smith. New York:
Charles Scribner's Sons, 1953.

_____. Hasidism and Modern Man. Edited and translated by
Maurice Friedman. New York: Harper and Row, 1958.

_____. A Believing Humanism: My Testament, 1902-1965.
New York: Simon and Schuster, 1967.

_____. Between Man and Man. Translated by Ronald Gregor
   Smith and Maurice Friedman. New York: Macmillan Co., 1970.

Castell, Alburey. The Self in Philosophy. New York: Macmillan
   Co., 1965.

Chambliss, Rollin. Social Thought: From Hammurabi to Conte.
   New York: Holt, Rinehart and Winston, 1954.

Churchman, C. West. Prediction and Optimal Decision: Philosophical Issues of a Science of Value. Englewood Cliffs:
   Prentice Hall, 1961.

Collins, James Daniel. The Mind of Kierkegaard. Chicago: Henry
   Regnery Co., 1953.

Cropley, A.J. Creativity. London: Longmans, Green and Co.,
   1967.

Dean, Edith, ed. All of the Women of the Bible. New York:
   Harper and Brothers, 1955.

Devine, Edward Thomas. When Social Work Was Young. New York:
   Macmillan Co., 1939.

Dewey, John. Democracy and Education. New York: Harper and
   Row, 1969.

Diamond, Malcolm Luria. Martin Buber: Jewish Existentialist.
   New York: Oxford Press, 1960.

Doniger, Simon, ed. The Nature of Man in Theological and Psychological Perspective. New York: Harper and Brothers, 1962.

Drucker, Peter F. The Age of Discontinuity. New York: Harper
   and Row, 1969.

Edwards, Jonathan. Christian Love and Its Fruits. Grand Rapids:
   Soverign Grace Publishers, 1971.

Eller, V. Kierkegaard and Radical Discipleship: A New
   Perspective. New Jersey: Princeton University Press, 1968.

Frankel, Charles. The Democratic Prospect. New York: Harper and
   Row, 1962.

Frankl, Viktor. The Doctor and the Soul. New York: Bantam

Books, 1969.

_____. Man's Search for Meaning: An Introduction to Logotherapy. New York: Washington Square Press, 1969.

_____. The Will to Meaning. New York: World Publishing Company, 1969.

Friedman, Maurice Stanley. Martin Buber: The Life of Dialogue. Chicago: University of Chicago Press, 1955.

_____. The Knowledge of Man. London: George Allen and Unwin, 1965.

Gordon, William J.J. Synectics. New York: Harper and Brothers, 1961.

Grene, Marjorie. The Knower and the Known. London: Faber and Faber, 1966.

Grene, Marjorie, ed. Knowing and Being: Essays by Michael Polanyi. London: Rutledge and Kegan Paul, 1969.

Hammond, Guyton. The Power of Self-Transcendence: An Introduction to Philosophical Theology of Paul Tillich. St. Louis: The Bethany Press, 1966.

Hastings, J., ed. Dictionary of the Bible. New York: Charles Scribner's Sons, 1963.

Hearn, Gordon. Theory Building in Social Work. Toronto: University of Toronto Press, 1958.

_____. The General Systems Approach: Contribution Toward an Holistic Conception of Social Work. New York: Council on Social Work Education, 1969.

Heidegger, Martin. Being and Time. Translated by J. Macquarrie and E. Robinson. New York: Harper and Row, 1962.

Heschel, Abraham J. Who is Man. Stanford: Stanford University Press, 1966.

Hoffman, Martin L., and Hoffman, Lois Wladis. Review of Child Development Research. Vol. 1, New York: Russell Sage Foundation, 1964.

The Holy Bible (King James Version). New York: The World
    Publishing Company, not dated.

Howard, Donald S. Social Welfare: Values, Means and Ends.
    New York: Random House, 1969.

Hume, David. Treatise of Human Nature. Oxford: Clarendon
    Press, 1896.

Husserl, Edmund. Cartesian Meditations: An Introduction to
    Phenomenology. Translated by Dorion Cairns. The Hague:
    Martinus Nijhoff, 1960.

_____. The Idea of Phenomenology. Translated by
    W.P. Alston and G. Nakmikian. The Hague: Martinus Nijhoff,
    1964.

James, William. The Principles of Psychology. Vol. 1. New York:
    Dover Publications, 1890.

Keith-Lucas, Alan. The Church and Social Welfare Philadelphia:
    Westminster Press, 1957.

Kierkegaard, Soren. Purity of Heart. Translated by Douglas V.
    Steere. New York: Harper and Brothers, 1948.

Kindelsperger, Walter L., ed. Social Process. Unpublished text-
    book. New Orleans: Tulane University School of Social
    Work, not dated.

King, Magda. Heidegger's Philosophy. New York: Macmillan Co.,
    1964.

Knight, Frank H., ed. Freedom and Reform. New York: Harper and
    Brothers, 1947.

Kohs, Samuel C. The Roots of Social Work. New York: Associated
    Press, 1966.

Langer, Susanne. Philosophy in a New Key. Cambridge,
    Massachusetts: Harvard University Press, 1967.

LeFevre, Perry D. The Prayers of Kierkegaard. Chicago:
    University of Chicago Press, 1956.

Lockyer, Herbert. All the Men of the Bible. Grand Rapids:
    Zondervan Publishing House, 1968.

Lockyer, Herbert. All the Women of the Bible. Grand Rapids: Zondervan Publishing House, 1967.

Longstreth, Longdon E. Psychological Development of the Child. New York: Ronald Press, 1968.

The Lutheran Church-Missouri Synod. Creation in Biblical Perspective: Report of the Commission on Theology and Church Relations. Not dated.

Lynd, Helen M. On Shame and the Search for Identity. New York: Harcourt, Brace and Co., 1958.

Martin, Bernard. Paul Tillich's Doctrine of Man. London: William Clowes and Sons, 1963.

Maslow, Abraham H. Motivations and Personality. New York: Harper and Brothers, 1954.

_____. Toward a Psychology of Being. New York: Van Nostrand Reinhold Co., 1968.

_____, ed. New Knowledge in Human Values. Chicago: Henry Regnery Co., 1970.

Matson, Floyd W., ed. Being, Becoming and Behavior: The Psychological Science. New York: George Braziller, 1967.

May, Rollo. Existence. New York: Simon and Schuster, 1958.

Mead, George Herbert. Mind, Self and Society. Edited by C.W. Morris. Chicago: University of Chicago Press, 1934.

Mead, Margaret, and Wolfenstein, Martha, eds. Childhood and Contemporary Culture. Chicago: University of Chicago Press, 1958.

Merleau-Ponty, Maurice. Phenomenology of Perception. Translated by C. Smith. New York: Humanities Press, 1962.

Miller, Seymour M., and Riessman, Frank. Social Class and Social Policy. New York: Basic Books, 1968.

Monteagu, Ashley. On Being Human. New York: Henry Schuman, 1951.

National Education Association. Perceiving, Behaving, Becoming.

Washington, DC: National Educational Association, 1962.

Overstreet, Harry Allen. Our Free Minds. New York: W.W. Norton and Co., 1941.

Perlman, Helen H. Social Casework: A Problem Solving Process. Chicago: University of Chicago Press, 1964.

Piaget, Jean. The Moral Judgment of the Child. Glencoe: Free Press, 1948.

Planck, Max Karl Ernest Ludwig. Where is Science Going. New York: W.W. Norton and Company, 1932.

Polanyi, Michael. Science, Faith and Society. London: Oxford University Press, 1946.

_____. Personal Knowledge. New York: Harper and Row, 1964.

Prochnow, Herbert V., ed. Great Stories from Great Lives. New York: Harper & Brothers Publisher, 1944.

Rank, Otto. Will Therapy and Truth and Reality. Translated by Jessie Taft. New York: Alfred A. Knopf, 1945.

Richmond, Mary E. Social Diagnosis. New York: Russell Sage Foundation, 1919.

_____. What is Social Casework. New York: Russell Sage Foundation, 1925.

Robinson, H. Wheeler. Suffering Human and Divine. New York: Macmillan Co., 1939.

Rogers, Carl R. Client-Centered Therapy. Boston: Houghton Mifflin Co., 1965.

_____. Freedom to Learn. Columbus, Ohio: Charles E. Merrill Publishing Co., 1969.

_____. Carl Rogers on Encounter Groups. New York: Harper & Row, 1970.

_____. Graduate Education in Psychology: A Passionate Statement. LaJolla: Western Behavioral Sciences Institute, not dated.

_____, and Stevens, Barry. _Person to Person._ New York: Pocket Books, 1971.

Russell, Bertrand. _Human Knowledge: Its Scope and Limits._ New York: Simon & Schuster, 1964.

Ryle, Gilbert. _The Concept of Mind._ London: Hutchinson House, 1951.

Sallis, John, ed. _Heidegger and the Path of thinking._ Pittsburgh: Duquesne University Press, 1970.

Sartre, Jean-Paul. _Of Human Freedom._ Edited by Wade Baskin. New York: Philosophical Library, 1966.

Skinner, B.F. _Science and Human Behavior._ New York: Macmillan Co., 1953.

_____. _Walden Two._ New York: Macmillan Co., 1962.

_____. _Beyond Freedom and Dignity._ New York: Alfred A. Knopf, 1972.

Smelser, Neil J., and Smelser, William T., eds. _Personality and Social Systems._ New York: John Wiley & Sons, 1965.

Sockman, Ralph W. _The Meaning of Suffering._ New York: Woman's Division of Christian Service, Board of Missions, The Methodist Church, 1961.

Sorokin, Pitrim A. _Altruistic Love._ Boston: Beacon Press, 1950.

Spiegelberg, Herbert. _The Phenomenological Movement._ Vol. 2. The Hague: Martinus Nijhoff, 1965.

Stein, Morris I., and Shirley, J. Heinze. _Creativity and the Individual._ Glencoe: Free Press, 1960.

Sumner, William Graham. _What Social Classes Owe to Each Other._ New York: Harper & Brothers, 1883.

Taylor, Alfred Edward. _Socrates._ New York: D. Appleton & Co., 1933.

Taylor, Calvin W. _Creativity_: Progress and Potential. New York: McGraw-Hill Book Co., 1964.
_____. _Widening Horizons in Creativity._ New York: John

Wiley & Sons, 1964.

Thomas, M. Women of the Bible. Nashville: Christian Family Books, 1964.

Tillich, Paul. The Courage To Be. New Haven: Yale University Press, 1953.

_____. Morality and Beyond: Religious Perspectives. Vol. 9. New York: Harper & Row, 1963.

_____. Systematic Theology I. Chicago: University of Chicago Press, 1965.

Torrence, E. Paul. Guiding Creative Talent. Englewood Cliffs: Prentice-Hall, 1962.

_____. Creativity: Its Educational Implications. New York: John Wiley & Sons, 1967.

_____. Creativity. San Rafael, California: Dimensions Publishing Co., 1969.

Torrey, R.A. The New Topical Textbook. Billy Graham Crusade Edition. Minnesota: World Wide Publications, not dated.

Tournier, Paul. The Meaning of Persons. London: Billing & Sons, 1965.

Vickers, Geoffrey. The Art of Judgment. New York: Basic Books, 1965.

Wheat, Leonard F. Paul Tillich's Dialectical Humanism: Unmasking the God above God. Baltimore: Johns Hopkins University Press, 1970.

Whitehead, Alfred North. The Aims of Education. New York: Macmillan Co., 1929.

_____. Adventures of Ideas. New York: Macmillan Co., 1956.

Wiener, Norbert. The Human Use of Human Beings. Boston: Houghton Mifflin Co., 1969.

Younghusband, Eileen, ed. Social Work and Social Values. London: George Allen & Unwin, 1967.

Articles

Allport, Gordon W. "Attitudes." In A Handbook of Social Psychology, edited by Carl Murchison. Worcester: Clark University Press, 1935.

_____. "Motivation in Personality: Reply to Mr. Bertocci." Psychological Review 47 (November, 1940): 533-554.

_____. "The Ego in Contemporary Psychology." Psychological Review 50 (September, 1943): 451-478.

_____. "Scientific Models and Human Morals." Psychological Review 54 (July, 1947): 182-192.

_____. "The Trend in Motivational Theory." American Journal of Orthopsychiatry 23 (January, 1953): 107-119.

_____. "The Open System in Personality Theory." Journal of Abnormal and Social Psychology 61 (November, 1960): 301-310.

Ansbacher, Heinz L. "Alfred Adler and Humanistic Psychology." Journal of Humanistic Psychology 11 (Spring, 1971): 53-63.

Aptekar, Herbert H. "Education for Social Responsibility." Journal of Education for Social Work 2 (Fall, 1966): 5-11.

Arieti, Silvano. "Toward a Unifying Theory of Cognition." General Systems 10 (1965): 109-115.

Arisian, Khoren, Jr. "Ethical Humanism and the Death of God." The Humanist 30 (Mar./Apr., 1970): 27-32.

Ausubel, David P. "Relationships Between Shame and Guilt in the Socialization Process." Psychological Review 62 (September, 1955): 379-390.

Baez, Joan; Campbell, J.; Ellis, A.; and Goodman, P. "The Authentic Man: A Symposium." The Humanist 30 (Jan./Feb., 1970): 19-26.

Banta, Thomas J. "Existentialism, Morality, and Psychotherapy." The Humanist 27 (Mar./Apr., 1967): 44-48.

Bergin, Allen E. "Psychology as a Science of Inner Experience."

Journal of Humanistic Psychology 4(Fall, 1964): 95-103.

Bertalanffy, Ludwig Von. "General Systems Theory." General Systems 1(1956): 1-10.

Blackburn, T.R. "Sensuous--Intellectual Complementarity in Science." Science, 4 June 1971, pp. 1003-1007.

Blumer, Herbert. "Society as Symbolic Interaction." In Human Behavior and Social Processes, edited by A. Rose. Boston: Houghton Mifflin Co., 1962.

Bronson, Louis H. "The Contributions of Virginia Robinson and Jessie Taft to Casework and Practice Theory." Mimeographed. University of Southern California School of Social Work, 21 November, 1967.

Bruner, Jerome S. "Culture, Politics, and Pedagogy." Saturday Review, 18 May 1968, pp. 69-72.

Bugental, James F.T. "Precognitions of a Fossel." Journal of Humanistic Psychology 2(Fall, 1962): 38-46.

_____. "The Third Force in Psychology." Journal of Humanistic Psychology 4 (Spring, 1964): 19-26.

_____. "The Challenge That is Man." Journal of Humanistic Psychology 7(Spring, 1967): 1-9.

_____. "The Humanistic Ethic--The Individual in Psychotherapy as a Societal Change Agent." Journal of Humanistic Psychology 11(Spring, 1971): 11-25.

Buhler, Charlotte. "The Human Course of Life in Its Goal Aspects." Journal of Humanistic Psychology 4(Spring, 1964): 1-17.

_____. "Some Observations on the Psychology of the Third Force." Journal of Humanistic Psychology 5(Spring, 1965): 54-55.

_____. "Human Life Goals in the Humanistic Perspective." Journal of Humanistic Psychology 7(Spring, 1967): 36-52.

Chein, Isidor. "The Awareness of Self and the Structure of the Ego." Psychological Review 51(September, 1944): 304-314.

Chenault, Joann. "Syntony: A Philosophical Premise for Theory and Research." Journal of Humainstic Psychology 6(Spring, 1966): 31-36.

Combs, Arthur W. "Phenomenological Concepts in Nondirective Therapy." Journal of Consulting Psychology 12(July/Aug., 1948): 197-208.

Crutchfield, Richard S. "The Creative Process." In Proceedings of the Institute of Personality Assessment and Research, University of California at Berkeley. Berkeley: University of California, 1961.

Day, Willard F. "Humanistic Psychology and Contemporary Behaviorism." The Humanist 31(Mar./Apr., 1971): 13-16.

Eysenck, H.J. "Reason with Comparison." The Humanist 31(Mar./Apr., 1971): 24-25.

Falck, Hans S. "Twentieth-Century Philosophy of Science and Social Work Education." Journal of Education for Social Work 6(Spring, 1970): 21-28.

Frankel, Charles. "The Moral Framework of the Idea of Welfare." In Welfare and Wisdom, edited by John S. Morgan. Toronto: University of Toronto Press, 1966.

_____. "Transformation of Welfare." In Welfare and Wisdom, edited by John S. Morgan. Toronto: University of Toronto Press, 1966.

_____. "The Relation of Theory to Practice." In Social Theory and Social Intervention, edited by H.D. Stein. Cleveland: The Press of Case Western Reserve University, 1968.

_____. "Social Values and Professional Values." Journal of Education for Social Work 5(Spring, 1969): 29-36.

Friedman, Maurice. "Existential Psychotherapy and the Image of Man." Journal of Humanistic Psychology 4(Fall, 1964): 104-117.

Fuller, R. Buckminster. "Commitment to Humanity." The Humanist 30(May/June, 1970): 28-33.

Glass, John F. "The Humanistic Challenge to Sociology." Journal of Humanistic Psychology 11(Fall, 1971): 170-183.

Graves, C. W. "Levels of Existence: An Open System Theory of Values." Journal of Humanistic Psychology 10(Fall, 1970): 131-155.

Greene, Maxine. "The Humanistic Challenge to Sociology." Journal of Education for Social Work 2(Spring, 1966): 21-31.

Guilford, J. P. "Creativity." American Psychologist 9(September, 1950): 444-454.

_____. "Three Faces of Intellect." In Readings in Classroom Learning, edited by Sherman H. Frey and Earl S. Haugen. New York: American Book Co., 1969.

Guzzetta, Charles. "Concepts and Percepts in Social Work Education. Journal of Education for Social Work 2(Fall, 1966): 40-47.

Handy, Rollo. "Ethics, Human Needs and Individual Responsibility." The Humanist 27(Jan./Feb., 1967): 11-14.

Huxley, Julian. "Transhumanism." Journal of Humanistic Psychology 8(Spring, 1968): 73-76.

Kadish, Sanford H. "The Theory of the Profession and Its Predicament." AAUP Bulletin 58(Summer, 1972): 120-125.

Kindelsperger, Walter L. "Responsible Entry into the Profession - Some Current Issues." Journal of Education for Social Work 2(Winter, 1965): 41-51.

King, Martin Luther. "The Future of Integration." The Humanist 28(Mar./Apr., 1968): 2-6.

Knowles, Malcolm S. "Innovations in Teaching Styles and Approaches Based on Adult Learning." Journal of Education for Social Work 8(Spring, 1972): 32-39.

Koch, Sigmund. "The Image of Man Implicit in Encounter Group Theory." Journal of Humanistic Psychology 11(Fall, 1971): 109-128.

Kurtz, Paul. "Humanism and the Freedom of the Individual." The Humanist 29(Jan./Feb., 1969): 14-19.

_____."The Moral Revolution: Toward a Critical Radicalism."
The Humanist 31(Mar./Apr., 1971): 4-5.

Kurtz, Paul; deFord, M.A.; and Zimmerman, M. "Definition of
Humanism." The Humanist 31(July/Aug., 1971): 4-5.

Lundholm, Helge. "Reflections upon the Nature of the
Psychological Self." Psychological Review 47(January, 1940):
110-127.

Mass, Henry S. "Social Work Knowledge and Social Responsibility."
Journal of Education for Social Work 4(Spring, 1968): 37-48.

MacCorquodale, Kenneth. "Behaviorism is a Humanism." The
Humanist 31(Mar./Apr., 1971): 12-13.

McCluer, F.L. "Keeping Our Freedom through Education." In
Proceedings of Council on Social Work Education, 1959: 7-9.

Markovic, Mihaila. "The Basic Characteristics of Marxist
Humanism." The Humanist 29(Jan./Feb., 1969): 19-23.

Maslow, Abraham H. "Notes on Being Psychology." Journal of
Humanistic Psychology 2(Fall, 1962): 47-71.

_____."A Theory of Metamotivation: The Biological Rooting of
the Value-Life." Journal of Humanistic Psychology 7(Fall,
1967): 93-127.

_____."Some Educational Implications of the Humanistic
Psychologies." Harvard Educational Review 38(Fall, 1968):
865-896.

_____."Peak Experiences in Education and Art." The Humanist
30(Sept./Oct., 1970): 29-30.

Matson, Floyd W. "Humanistic Theory: The Third Revolution in
Psychology." The Humanist 31(Mar./Apr., 1971): 7-11.

May, Rollo. "Intentionality, the Heart of Human Will." Journal
of Humanistic Psychology 5(Fall, 1965): 202-209.

McBride, Esther Barnhart. "A Re-Evaluation of Assumptions
Commonly Held about Changing Societies." Paper presented in
a graduate course in sociology at Tulane University, New
Orleans, January 1966. Typed.

Meyer, Donald H. "The Scientific Humanism of Stanley Hall."
Journal of Humanistic Psychology 11(Fall, 1971): 201-213.

Miano, V. "Meaning and Limits of Christian Humanism." The
Humanist 31(May/June, 1971): 31-33.

Miller, Henry. "Value Dilemma in Social Casework." Social Work
13(January, 1968): 27-33.

Moustakas, Clark. "The Sense of Self." Journal of Humanistic
Psychology 1(Spring, 1961): 20-34.

_____."Honesty, Idiocy, and Manipulation." Journal of
Humanistic Psychology 2(Fall, 1962): 1-15.

Nameche, Gene F. "Two Pictures of Man." Journal of Humanistic
Psychology 1(Spring, 1961): 70-88.

Norris, Louis William. "Men of Principle." Saturday Review 18
November, 1961, p. 48.

Polanyi, Michael. "Scientific Outlook: Its Sickness and Cure."
Science 125(1957): 480-484.

Progoff, I. "Toward a Depth Humanistic Psychology." Journal of
Humanistic Psychology 10(Fall, 1970): 121-130.

Ricks, David F., and Wessman, Alden E. "WINN: A Case of a Happy
Man." Journal of Humanistic Psychology 6(Spring, 1966):
2-16.

Rogers, Carl R. "Some Observations on the Organization of
Personality." American Psychologist 2(September, 1947):
358-365.

_____."Persons of Science? A Philosophical Question."
American Psychologist 10(July, 1955): 267-278.

_____."A Theory of Therapy, Personality, and Interpersonal
Relationships, as Developed in the Client-Centered
Framework." In Psychology: A Study of a Science, edited by
S. Koch. New York: McGraw-Hill Book Co., 1959.

_____."Toward a Science of the Person." Journal of Humanistic
Psychology 3(Fall, 1963): 72-92.

_____. "Some Questions and Challengers Facing a Humanistic

Psychology." Journal of Humanistic Psychology 5 (Spring, 1965): 1-5.

Rogers, Carl R., and Skinner, B.F. "Some Issues Concerning the Control of Human Behavior: A Symposium." Science, 30 November, 1956, pp. 1057-1066.

Rose, A.M. "A Systematic Summary of Symbolic Interaction Theory." In Human Behavior and Social Processes, edited by A.M. Rose. Boston: Houghton Mifflin Co., 1962.

Schachtel, E.G. "On Creative Experience." Journal of Humanistic Psychology 11 (Spring, 1971): 26-39.

Seward, John P. "The Sign of a Symbol: A Reply to Professor Allport." Psychological Review 55 (September, 1948): 277-296.

Skinner, B.F. "Utopia and Human Behavior." The Humanist 37 (July/Aug., 1967): 136-138.

_____. "Humanistic Behaviorism." The Humanist 31 (May/June, 1971): 35.

_____. "Humanism and Behaviorism." The Humanist 32 (July/Aug., 1972): 18-20.

Smillie, David. "The Roots of Personal Existence." Journal of Humanistic Psychology 1 (Spring, 1961): 89-93.

Smith, M. Brewster. "The Phenomenological Approach in Personality Theory: Some Critical Remarks." Journal of Abnormal and Social Psychology 45 (July, 1950): 516-522.

Strodtbeck, Fred L. "Family Interaction, Values and Achievement." In Talent and Society, edited by David C. McClelland; Alfred L. Bronfendrenner; and Fred L. Strodtbeck. New York: D. Van Nostrand Co., 1958.

Sutich, Anthony J. "Transpersonal Psychology: An Emerging Force." Journal of Humanistic Psychology 8 (Spring, 1968): 77-78.

Tart, Charles T., and Creighton, James L. "The Bridge Mountain Community: An Evolving Pattern for Human Growth." Journal of Humanistic Psychology 6 (Spring, 1966): 56-67.

Thompson, T. Gale, and O'Donovan, Danis. "Control, Freedom and Science" Journal of Humanistic Psychology 5(Spring, 1965): 70-81.

Torrance, E. Paul. "Exploration in Creative Thinking." In Readings in Classroom Learning, edited by Sherman H. Frey and Earl S. Haugen. New York: American Book Co., 1969.

Towle, Charlotte. "Implication of Contemporary Human and Social Values for Student Selection." In Proceedings of Council on Social Work Education (1959): 25-38.

Troutner, LeRoy F. "The Confrontation Between Experimentalism and Existentialism: From Dewey through Heidegger and Beyond." Harvard Educational Review 39(Winter, 1969): 124-155.

Warmoth, Arthur. "A Note on the Peak-Experience as a Personal Myth." Journal of Humanistic Psychology 5(Spring, 1965): 18-21.

Watts, A. "Oriental and Occidental Approaches to the Nature of Man." Journal of Humanistic Psychology 2(Fall, 1962): 107-109.

Winthrop, Henry. "Self-Sacrifice as Autonomy, Ego-Transcendence and Social Interest." Journal of Humanistic Psychology 2(Fall, 1962): 31-37.

Witte, Ernest F. "A World We Never Made." In Social Work: Promise and Promises, edited by Sue Spencer. Nashville: University of Tennessee School of Social Work, 1968.

SUPPLEMENTARY BIBLIOGRAPHY

Adler, Mortimer J. The Difference of Man and the Difference It Makes. 1st ed. New York: Holt, Rinehart & Winston, 1967.

deChardin, Teilhard. The Phenomenon of Man. Translated by Bernard Wall, with an introduction by Julian Huxley. New York: Harper Torchbooks, 1959.

May, Rollo; Angel, Ernest; and Ellenberger, Henri F. Existence: A Dimension in Psychology and Psychiatry. New York: Basic Books, 1968.